By the same author:

Steam Sapper (1992)
ISBN 1 872017 51 7

Living with Locos

LNER Footplate Memories

Charles Meacher was born in the post office at Dalmeny Village, West Lothian, where his mother was postmistress, on 15th May 1920.

He was educated at Bellevue School (now Drummond High) in Edinburgh and joined the London and North Eastern Railway in 1935 as a locomotiveman.

During World War II he served with the Royal Engineers on docks and railways at home and abroad.

On cessation of hostilities Charles returned to the LNER, later BR, and served over the years as fireman, driver, inspector, running foreman, and accident reporting officer, from which post he retired in 1987 having completed 48 years railway service.

St Margarets MIC team, consistent winners of British
Rail contests. The picture shows Driver Frank Mitchell
(Captain) accepting the Shield with a handshake from
M.C. Ross Campbell, Motive Power Superintendent.
From left to right: Tom Philbin, John Bruce,
Michael Flaherty, M.C. Ross Campbell, Frank
Mitchell, George Shearer, Tom Nimmo.

SMOKE, STEAM AND WHISTLES

Charles Meacher

A Square One Publication

First published by Square One Publications
Saga House, Sansome Place, Worcester, WR1 1UA

© Charles Meacher 1993

British Library Cataloguing in Publication Data
is available for this title

Smoke, Steam and Whistles

ISBN: 1 872017 74 6

Typeset by Avon Dataset, Bidford on Avon, Warwickshire B50 4JH
Printed in England by Biddles Ltd, Guildford

The average person has a story to relate but most people think their life is too humdrum to be of interest to others. There seems no excitement in watching bottles or packages passing on a conveyor belt; laying bricks is repetition with a capital "R"; sweeping streets is a thankless chore especially when someone drops litter in your wake. Yet with some imagination and human interest all such menial tasks are material for books.

The work of an author writing about steam locomotives is made easy, such is the abiding interest in a machine identifiable with humankind. This hissing, fire-eating, volcanic image has to be regularly fed and watered with no undue retention of waste or arterial blockage. When "off colour" and performing poorly a driver will urge his steam engine on to greater effort just as football supporters afford verbal encouragement to their favourite team.

The steam engine is feminine gender and in conversation enginemen can be heard to say "she's a guid yin" or, conversely, "that bitch couldn't steam between two telegraph poles". Of course, drivers and firemen lacking experience with a particular breed of locomotive can contribute to the engine's inefficiency.

This book deals with fundamentals, servicing and main-tenance as well as the human effort required to operate a steam railway. The "locomotive vapore", as the steam locomotive is known in Italy, in its declining years was not far removed from the Victorian environment into which it was born. Working conditions at St Margarets NBR/LNER/BR depot in Edin-burgh and the habitat changed hardly at all in its 120 years existence from 1846 – 1966.

For maximum pleasure in reading this book the reader should lie back with feet on mantelpiece allowing warm air to radiate from fire to buttocks, the rump, or hind part of the anatomy. Hopefully, in this way, he will experience the sensation of rather more than ordinary heat such as the warmth dissemi-nated by a steam locomotive.

Preface

Although this book depicts primarily the NBR/LNER steam scene in Scotland, the story is typical of steam train work throughout Britain. The ruggedness of the steam locomotive was often mirrored in the character of the men who put life into these fascinating machines. Some drivers felt wedded to a particular engine and the sentiment of Haymarket driver James Paterson on retiral was not unique. He had the Gresley A4 No 60009 for 12 years and as he cast a fond gaze over his shoulder in "No 9's" direction he said to his friends, "Yes, I loved that engine like a man loves a woman".

It is to Jim and his like I dedicate this book. I know exactly how he felt.

Nor do I forget the real women who made up "pieces" and tea bottles at all hours of the day and night, and continually boosted the morale of "enginemen elite" and enginemen anonymous. Such devotion will long be remembered and appreciated.

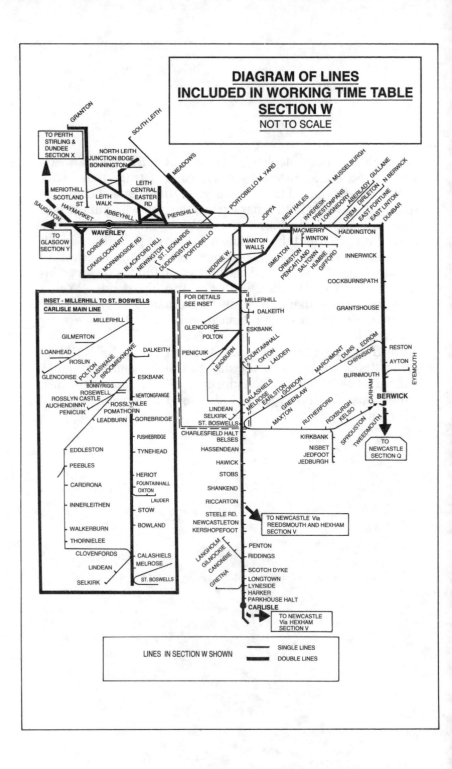

DIAGRAM OF LINES
INCLUDED IN WORKING TIME TABLE
SECTION W
NOT TO SCALE

INSET - MILLERHILL TO ST. BOSWELLS
CARLISLE MAIN LINE

LINES IN SECTION W SHOWN — SINGLE LINES / DOUBLE LINES

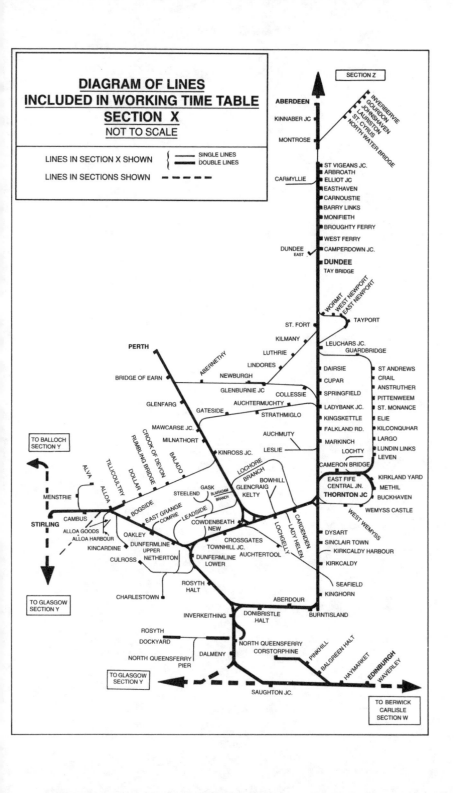

Chapter 1

Servicing the Steam Locomotive

It was a rare event when an engine arriving at St Margarets M.P.D had room to move in the coal store. Usually, this fuelling stage was chock-a-block with many types of loco which made up an allocation of some 220 engines. If there was room in the coal store an engine arriving just buffered up to the queue already there, but if the road was empty or near empty a gaffer would be there waving a desperately needed engine to a particular tip.

There were 8 tips at St Margarets but only two in normal use, No 6 and No 8. Big tender engines, after taking on coal at No 6 would move to a higher level at No 8 where the tender was 'topped up'.

Four sets of men (driver & fireman) were employed on disposal work non-stop, while 'spare' drivers were utilized to 'shove up' ie, keep the coal store on the move and see to fires and boiler water level.

It was important for St Margarets to have a supply of large coals to facilitate shovelling and tender filling. Small coals required more shovel work and a box of these 'nuts' made little impression on an empty Pacific tender. The coalmen were on bonus and were paid tonnage money so they preferred big lumps.

These coalmen wore only a light singlet over their muscular frame and could be likened to miners. St Margarets coal stage was difficult to work because wagon doors had to be removed to get at the coal. In Carlisle London Road for instance, the steel stage plates were at wagon wheel level and doors could be opened and dropped allowing coal to cascade and fill two or more ½-ton tubs.

1

St Margarets coalmen had to unfasten hinge nuts and remove wagon door before shovelling.

After claiming a particular wagon the coalmen removed the wagon ticket and put it in a safe place. The tonnage on that ticket would confirm amount of work done when the coal clerk checked same and arranged payment. Eight tons of coal had to be shovelled before tonnage money was payable. If at the end of a shift a coalman left a 'part load' this was shunted out and brought back for the man next day. Empty wagons were used for ash disposal and included a great deal of coal overlooked by coalmen.

St Margarets was fully dependent on good coal servicing and when at times two Gresley Pacifics filled the coal store and denied entry to smaller engines arrangements were made to have the big engines coaled mechanically at Haymarket. Usually, the men who took these engines to 64B were instructed to prepare them for particular jobs and on return to St Margarets trainmen took over on the mainline and went to Niddrie, Portobello, or, South Leith, wherever the engines were required. They were also turned at Haymarket, if necessary.

Not only the coalmen held the key to success at St Margarets the tipper could put 'a spoke in the wheels', as the saying goes. I have seen the whole place at a standstill when a certain tipper 'took the pet' and sulked. This was because the wheels on the ½-ton tubs had not been oiled making them less easy to push. A labourer was supposed to do the oiling but usually it was the gaffer labourer who did the job and if he was not available or had forgotten, work came to a halt.

Sometimes, things would be going so well there was a shortage of empty tubs. Then we would see coalmen tipping their own tubs and working like trojans to maximise earnings.

When too much effort was put into tipping, a tub would end up in an engine tender. The engine would then be moved alongside lower ground and volunteers would man-handle the heavy box and drop it over the side. Next day, a crane returned the box to the coal stage.

2

Between shifts engines had a long stand in the coal store and fires and water level had to be attended. One set of disposal men were booked out half an hour later than the others and these "half hour" men were on hand at the change of shifts to do the odd shunt or whatever was necessary.

On one occasion when I was "half hour" driver I was told to turn the Class A4 No 60019 Bittern and dispose of this engine. The approach to the 70 ft turntable was on a curve and as Bittern's wheels bit into the rails I kept pumping steam to keep her moving with short jabs of the steam regulator. Suddenly, the A4 became the A3 No 60081 and "Shotover" the turntable burying its nose in the rock face housing the turntable.

After turning the A4 I took it on shed for examination and subsequently there was only slight damage to cylinder cocks. I put in a repair card and Bittern was fit and well for her next job, the 5.19 pm ex Leith Walk "brakes" loaded with whisky and tobacco destined for London, Kings Cross.

St Margarets had two ash lyes No 10 and No 12 with a gully, No 11, in between. This gully held about nine ash wagons which made easy downwards shovelling for the daytime ash squad. Many of these men were casuals and unknown quantities. It was not unusual for them to sub their wages at midweek and disappear from the scene before repayment was due on Friday. St Margarets experimented for some time with a mechanical grab for loading ashes but mostly it was human effort that shovelled ashes.

There were tenement houses in proximity and threatening women at the windows to remind workers about smoke nuisance. A class 2 supervisory post was specially created to watch the situation and the men cleaning fires and smoke boxes. As red hot ashes spewed from fire boxes the gaffer would be hosing this lava as it streamed to the ground, causing clouds of dirt laden steam and a terrible stink when the place was used as a urinal.

The firedroppers and "smokers" shared a bothy and

3

took it in turns to deal with locos as they arrived. There was a big blackboard on the wall and these men would chalk their names on this board and list the engines dealt with. If a firebox or smoke box was not properly cleaned it was a simple matter for the shift gaffer to check the engine number against blackboard numbers and identify the culprit. This dodger then had to get a wheelbarrow and go to the engine in the shed and complete the job.

There was usually only one ashpan man, a very dirty job which called for a face mask and close fitting clothes. In practice, however, the ashpan man usually got stuck into the job, regardless. Wee Andrew Elder was like this, always smiling and cracking jokes as he raked hot ashes (and coals) from the belly of a Pacific and a drop-grate. No matter which way the wind was blowing Andrew was as happy as a pig in a pigsty. In these circumstances some ashpan men would call for the engine to be turned.

A smokers job was also exceedingly dirty and his collar and trouser ends would be tightly bound. Binding the trouser ends was also a safety measure. One unfortunate smoke box cleaner was preparing to jump to the ground instead of using fixed steps provided. He didn't see a fixed lamp holder was up his trouser leg and when he jumped this caused retardment and the smoker fell clumsily and broke his neck. He never worked again and wore a surgical collar ever afterwards.

Being common users St Margarets high capacity engines were in a deplorable condition. It was quite a sight to stand and watch a K3, Green Arrow or Pacific having its smokebox cleaned. Very often a smokebox door would be burnt and when it was opened there appeared a solid mass of hot ashes as high as the chimney petticoat being waffed by outside air and glowing red.

Immediately below the chimney the blastpipe had created a deep narrow hole yet the black mass of ashes remained in place hiding from sight a honeycomb of boiler tubes. Ashes had fallen from behind the baffle plate in the smoke box door but a great amount was still lodged in this recess. In order to expel the trapped ashes the smoke box cleaner would bang on the door with his shovel causing a cascade and leaving him ankle deep in cinders.

Then he had to face up to the main exercise and dig his shovel into the solid wall of burnt ashes inside the smoke box. This disturbance would cause a collapse of the ash pile but there was no escape from this greater cascade since the engine was on a pit and the ground many feet away. The sensible practice to adopt was to use a long iron poker and dislodge the ashes before going near the smoke box to shovel this deposit. Whatever way it was done it was drudgery and dirt with capital d's. A smoker's delight was to see an engine with "SC" on the smoke box — Self Cleaner.

This device avoids the accumulation of ashes in the smoke box and evens the effect of the blast over the whole tubeplate, preventing the emission of sparks thrown up the chimney. Deflecting and diaphragm plates with front spark arrester or ash plate are fitted. The vertical diaphragm plate in front of the tube plate ensure that an equal draught passes through the tubes.

The self cleaning action is attained by locating the horizontal table plate just under the top flange of the blast pipe and setting the redirection plate at such an angle as, combined with sufficient area of netting, will allow for the free steaming of the locomotive. The diaphragm plates cause the ashes, drawn through the tubes, to transverse the lower part of the smoke box through a restricted opening; the ashes are then drawn through a wire net screen before being harmlessly ejected through the chimney.

Apart from the chimney orifice a smoke box should be airtight but if the door is not properly closed and sealed it can draw air. This is what causes the hot ashes to burn the inside of the door and in darkness this burning glows red and is readily seen while in daylight the damage appears as a white or brown blotch.

The usual fittings in a smoke box include superheater header (when fitted) main steam pipes, blower and ejection exhaust pipes. On some locomotives the regulator valve is situated in the superheater header in the smoke

5

box. There is also the all important tube plate. To reach these for repair purposes means removing SC plates and cages so fitters and boilersmiths and boiler washers have some preparation work to do before starting a job properly.

Firedropping is hard, hot work especially if there is no drop grate. It was easy to turn a handle and let the fire drop into a pit but using a long shovel to haul it through a firedoor is a different matter. Unless the dander shovel (as we called it) was well tempered it soon buckled with the heat and became useless. To reach the 'back of the door' a bent poker with a half moon blade was used to push the fire forward then the fire was removed with the long dander shovel. It was like a fireworks display to see these glowing hot ashes being thrown from the engine cab at night.

The drop-grate was advantageous but it could cause trouble and seize up. In this case the boilersmith would take over and maybe effect a repair. If not, the engine had to be stopped and cooled down until a repair could be done.

Chapter 2

The Locomotive Boiler

Apart from washing out boilers at regular intervals there was also periodical boiler inspection. St Margarets would be advised that certain engines had to be made available on a certain date for boiler inspection. This meant the engines had to be thoroughly cleaned, smoke box, fire box and ashpan. The numbers were marked in the log book and on the black board in firedroppers bothy and the gaffer would tell everybody concerned "mind, that's a BI". This was also chalked on cabside so there was no excuse for slip-ups.

When the Boiler Inspector appeared he was like a man from outer-space, wearing hooded boilersuit, with tools and portable lamp at the ready. Every stay and plug in the boiler was tapped and closely examined, every firebar checked; tenders, too, were his prerogative. Boilersmiths were on their toes when the boiler inspector visited and he wasn't slow to reprimand the maintenance men if there was cause to do so.

Boiler washing was important work at steam engine sheds and a boiler washer and mate could expect three engines on each shift — day shift, back shift, night shift at St Margarets. A record was kept in the running office so that an engine would become due for washing out every twelve days or so. When there was an acute shortage of power, not unusual at St Margarets it was frustrating to see an engine coming on shed then realise it was due a wash-out (WO). This was chalked on the cab side and on the board in the firedroppers bothy as well as the engine board. It was important to fitters because much work could be carried out while the engine was stopped. If a 64A loco was out with its territory for a long period the sure way to get it back home was to tell Control engine was overdue washout. Control would then trace it and send a wire "Ohio — all speed Engine 60970, overdue washout". "Ohio" being the code word for return to home depot. Next day, or the day after No 60970 would come limping back from the North Eastern Region or even Kings Cross in a terrible mess.

There was a stationary boiler at steam sheds to supply hot water under pressure for washing out purposes. This water was piped by flexible hose to the boiler being dealt with. The boiler washer on site would control water supply by a tarzan-like call to his mate positioned at the stopcock. This jungle call was necessary to distinguish it from other noises in the shed.

Sometimes a big boiler could not be cleaned in one shift because of "dirty barrel". This meant the boiler barrel inside the steel shell was solid with sludge and scale, hard to shift. There is also the outer firebox wrapper plate, back plate, throat plate and smoke box tube plate also the inner firebox and the steel flue tubes.

On a tapered boiler the cylindrical barrel is made in two sections with the longer diameter at the rear, where the barrel is joined to the outer firebox. The dome which houses the regulator valve and auxiliary internal steam pipes is positioned on top of the boiler barrel where it forms a collector for steam above the surface of the water. It is not, as some people used to say, intended to make the engines look tippy, or smart.

The inner firebox is supported from the outer firebox by the foundation ring at the bottom, by crown stays at the top and by palm stays between the firebox tube plate and the boiler barrel. In addition, the firebox and outer wrapper plates, back plate and throat plate are stayed together with steel or copper stays, at about 4 in pitch; there are over 1000 of these stays in every locomotive boiler.

Longitudinal stays are also fitted between the boiler

back plate and smokebox tube plate, and cross stays between the sides of the outer wrapper plate above the firebox crown. From the firebox tube plate, the steel flue tubes, which may be anything from 1½ in to 2¼ in, diameter, pass through the boiler barrel to the smokebox tube plate. When the boiler is fitted with a superheater, a number of large flue tubes (approximately 5 in diameter) are provided in which superheater elements are positioned. Some boilers employ the flat-top type of firebox. The boiler barrel and firebox are lagged with asbestos or glass wool. It is normal practice in Britain for inner fireboxes to be made of copper but there are instances when steel fireboxes are used.

It is readily apparent that a steam locomotive boiler is a complex structure with many crevices to harbour scale and dirt. Hot water under pressure dislodges this residue which is released through mud doors located at low level to allow clearance by gravity and a poke with a long, flexible steel rod. The red scale falls with the water into the inspection pit and surrounding area and is swept up eventually at the daily sweeping of shed roads.

Mud doors are designed to tighten against the inside of the boiler and have suitable jointing to ensure a tight fit. Sometimes when the engine makes steam a mud door joint or washout plug on wrong thread may be seen to blow. This calls for a decision by the boilersmith who may tighten the plug or mud door under pressure or "order all fire out". Some boildersmiths were more daring than others especially when urged on by an impatient running foreman.

Missing firebars had sometimes to be replaced on a locomotive with small fires burning. This was usually done with the use of tongs to grip the firebars being manoeuvred into place. But, I remember on one occasion at Carlisle Canal shed a boilersmith climbed in beside the hot coals on a Class A3 Pacific and did a quick, very quick repair. The lip of the firebox mouth was very hot and he covered this with thick sacking then slid like an eel into the firebox. He was soon out again, his face and hands red like beetroot.

At St Margarets there was a man washing out boilers with the nickname "Monty". He had been on the victory parade in Tunis and as Field Marshall Montgomery inspected the ranks he stood before the 64A man and said "Well my man — are you proud?" "Yes, indeed, sir" replied the soldier. Then Montgomery spoke again, "If anyone asks what you did in the war tell them you marched with Montgomery". After a story like that the boiler washer just had to be called Monty.

An engine with Walschearts' valve gear had to be set to allow access to washout plugs behind the gear and lower framing. This setting usually came right as washout engines were stabled but sometimes a move was required to facilitate access to plugs.

Monty was always early on the job to get an early finish and it was not unusual for him to intercept the running foreman as this worthy crossed the main line to tackle the problems synonymous with St Margarets. Usually a gaffer would tell Monty to "get lost, I've more to think about than your wash-out engines". When acting foreman I looked at the situation differently thinking, "The quicker Monty gets a move the quicker the W.O. engines will be ready for kindling". So, I would immediately detail men to give Monty a shunt and let him get on with his work.

The same applied to fitters requiring a move, my aim was to get engines back into traffic as quickly as possible.

Chapter 3

Heroes and Hazards

Construction of St Margarets locomotive works and shed coincided with the opening of the North British Railways main line to Berwick in June 1846. In my time the place had had 100 years to deteriorate and this degeneration showed in many ways. The shed roof was in a sad state of disrepair and four foot thick walls did nothing to shelter man and engines since most of the huge windows had never been glazed since installation. This former carriage shed had six dead end roads and in daytime it would be empty, airy and ugly. The lyes between pits were of red brick construction and rarely repaired. There were years of grease and dirt all around and baked soot holding the rafters together. Supporting pillars went unpainted and an occasional application of whitewash on the walls was a joke.

At night time all this ugliness was hidden by dense smoke from engines packed solid in every road. On a Sunday night when engines were kindled the reek was unbearable and work impossible. This meant cleaners and fitters had to work in the open and if weather was inclement men would huddle and lounge in the many bothies available.

Engine disposal men, drivers and firemen, didn't have a bothy, they congregated close to a furnace which served to dry sand and supply kindling for lighting engine fires. As the enginemen stood in a group sheltering from rain, snow or wind a steamraiser would disturb them as he dug his scoop into the fire for kindling. Then with his back to the furnace he would hoist the hot coals on to his shoulder and swing round to his direction of travel. This circular sweep of fire made the enginemen scatter and someone would be heard to say "oh, bugger this, I'm going up on an engine" and the disturbed soul would retire to an engine cab to sit in peace.

The steamraisers' 'hod' as one might call it was an ordinary firing shovel with high sides and long shaft. As he carried this to a dead engine the glow could be followed as he progressed and if it was windy he trailed showers of sparks.

In winter when snow and ice prevailed St Margarets became a winter wonderland. Braziers full of flaming fire were positioned at every water point and between rows of engines to prevent water injectors and brake gearing freezing up. These hot fires were also up on the coal-stage to temper the cold air that threatened to freeze the workers on that high perch. It was hot work shovelling coal but when standing idle with only a thin vest and shapeless trousers to guard against extreme cold a blazing fire could be warming and welcome.

In summer time these braziers lay rusting on site and usually upside down with legs in the air. Close to the old roundhouse on the north side one very dark night a fireman climbed down from a tender after filling a tank. He did not see the upturned brazier on the ground and as he lowered his body a brazier leg penetrated his anus and caused injury.

Incomers at St Margarets had to be extra careful. I remember a driver newly arrived from Burntisland was turning a pug in the old shed one day. As he pushed the 42 ft turntable he was unaware, or forgot, the limited clearance between moving turntable and stabled engines and he was crushed to death between turntable and engine buffer.

Another fatality involved a driver from Eastfield. He had watched the departure of a Class V3 engine from the coal store road and rightly expected this engine to come up the straight line adjacent to where he stood in the "four foot", but someone failed to pull the points and the V3 came back into the coal store road knocking the Eastfield man down. A local doctor crawled under the engine to give medical attention but to no avail, the Glasgow man died.

Considering its potential for accidents there were surprisingly few such happenings over the years. I was at Haymarket as a telephone boy when I learned of a serious accident at St Margarets. Jimmy Sinclair, a popular gaffer, had been talking with a Haymarket driver, Lawrie Daniels, who stood with his train of empty coaches en route Waverley station on the down line at St Margarets. When the Home signal cleared and the train moved away Jimmy Sinclair on the level crossing walked behind the departing train and into the path of the Up Flying Scotsman. Such fierce kinetic energy caused instant death and, as was usual in those days, P'way men had to pick up the pieces.

Years later death came to Jimmy Rooney, a St Margarets driver, in a similar fashion. Rooney was taking a short cut over the main line not far from the spot where Sinclair died. As Rooney crawled between wagons he failed to see a Down express from Carlisle approaching and stood up in the path of this fast train accelerating for the climb to Waverley Station.

On shed, an ever present danger was fouled crossing boards at the mouth of the shed. With space at a premium it was common though irregular practice for engine buffers to foul these boards and people would squeeze through the narrow space rather than walk a long way around or climb through an engine cab.

David MacFarlane, a gland packer, took a chance one day and trod the crossing board just as the buffers closed up. David became trapped as if in a vice and when the engines were parted his dead body dropped to the ground.

Poor lighting and fouled footpaths made St Margarets a danger zone in darkness. Sometimes, the glow from an engine fire would identify a hazard, a shovel or a poker, a lamp, or a heap of coal lying in wait for the unwary. Another danger was passing an engine cab when a fireman was spraying hot water to keep the dust down. It wasn't very nice to receive an earful of hot water under pressure, causing howls of protest. One was just as likely to be struck by a red hot poker as a fireman swung this through the air and on to the rack on the tender. While congratulating oneself in avoiding such horror it was possible to be drenched in wet soot as a vacuum ejector was opened without warning. This happened when a driver testing his vacuum brake opened the steam ejector which created vacuum. All the soot in the smokebox would be blasted high and rain down on everybody in the vicinity.

Most enginemen were considerate and gave adequate warning of danger. Throughout the day and night there were cries of "all clear of engine so and so" a preliminary warning engine "so and so" was about to be moved.

There were "not to be moved" boards affixed to engines under repair or being cleaned. The kind of shunts taking place in St Margarets required great stopping distance. With possibly six engines of various types to control and very little steam for brake power a driver needed plenty warning to stop. Usually, the foreman as well as the fireman was in attendance to guide the convoy into the shed or to outside roads. A breach of safety rules that persisted for years was the use of No 6 road for live engines. This is where the wheel drop was installed and engines in this road were usually minus a pair of wheels which would be under repair in the machine shop, having tyres refixed or axle boxes repaired. The only live engine allowed into No 6 road was for shunting purposes.

The location of No 6 road in relation to ash disposal lyes made it a convenient depository for all sizes of engines, there was usually no need to ask the signalman for a shunt on the main line and this alone was an advantage in getting on with the work. It was also helpful if an engine low in steam and brake power limped on to the shed. There was room to use the reverser as a brake and run forward into No 6 road. This was also adjacent to the sand kiln and furnace so kindling was at hand to fill up the firebox and raise steam, and buckets of sand didn't have to be carried far in preparation work. It was when these engines moved into the shed and got too near to the wheel drop that fitters panicked and threatened to stop work.

If wheels required a great deal of attention they were loaded into a special wheel wagon and sent to Cowlairs Works in Glasgow. There was also a stores van in use for distributing locomotive material between Cowlairs and Motive Power Depots on the former NBR system. This van was marshalled next to the loco and went to the shed with the loco after working a passenger train. Carlisle Canal, St Margarets, Haymarket and Eastfield were all served in this way and each depot had its own receptacle for locomotive spare parts in the van.

The first mention of St Margarets depot was made in January 1846, when 14 engines obtained by the NBR from Hawthorn of Newcastle were stored there pending the opening of the railway six months later. The first locomotive superintendent was Robert Hawthorn who had been in charge of the Haymarket depot of the Edinburgh and Glasgow Railway

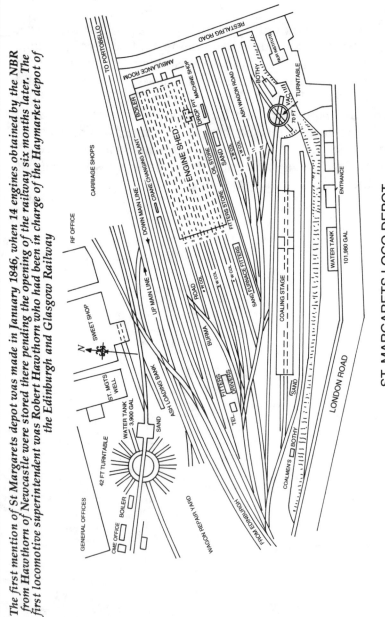

ST. MARGARETS LOCO DEPOT

Chapter 4

Knowledge is Power

St Margarets had a very active Mutual Improvement Class where enginemen were tutored for promotion. After studying valves and gearing on a model it was helpful to visit the fitting shop and see the real thing. The Stephenson vale gear, for instance, took on new meaning when one viewed a Class J37 stripped down at close quarters. The cylinders hidden inside the framing under the smokebox were like huge dark caverns and one readily realised the great power those 19½" × 26" bores were capable of. A driver at the controls seldom thinks of what is making the wheels go round, his main concern is that they do go round and the fireman maintains steam pressure.

Turning to another loco under repair the trainee driver could gain intimate knowledge of the Walschaerts valve gear. On a Pacific engine with this gear you can stand on the ground and put your head in the empty cylinder and see where the steam comes in and goes out. It doesn't take a lot of imagination to see a huge piston being pushed to and fro linked to the wheels to impart movement. The piston itself is lying on the ground having carbon removed and rings cleaned. These rings are about 5/16 in. in width and their flexible design ensures a steam tight movement along cylinder walls.

Climb up to the front of this engine and the open smokebox door is like an invitation to look inside. This is an extension of the boiler barrel which together with the blast pipe and chimney, forms the means of inducing air, required for combustion, to the firebox. Other fittings include superheater header which distributes steam from the boiler to a series of superheating tubes (or elements) and receives superheated steam from the elements. The superheater header is attached by a flanged joint to the smokebox tubeplate at the outlet of the main internal steam pipe from the regulator valve and is placed horizontally across the upper part of the smokebox. At each side of the header are flanges to which are attached the main steam pipes to the cylinder.

The header casting is divided into saturated and superheated compartments. Steam passing from the regulator valve in the main internal steam pipe can only reach the cylinders by traversing the superheater elements connecting the two compartments in the header, the elements forming the only communication between the two separate sections. The number of superheater elements installed varies according to the size of the boiler and the degree of superheat required.

This means of drying saturated steam and greatly increasing its temperature and power was tried out by the NBR in February 1911 when Schmidt superheaters were ordered for two Scott Class engines under construction, No 400 The Dugal Cratur and No 303 Hal o' the Wynd. It was a major advance in the development of the steam locomotive resulting in great economy of coal and water and labour.

The superheater elements were installed in large flu tubes extending between the firebox and smokebox with only bifurcated ends showing. Outside in the yard, however, the whole element could be viewed in a lean-to shed when they were shelved alongside tubes.

Damage could be caused to these elements through running for long periods with steam shut off. Their existence, of course, made extra work for boilersmiths but nothing compared with the work performance of firing a saturated steam engine. I never experienced such work but I know a generation of firemen who had sweated with these coal and water gobblers on the tortuous Aberdeen and Waverley routes.

It was important that boiler tubes should be kept clean and a man, a tuber, was employed at St Margarets for this purpose. It was a dirty job and the tuber had to be suitably attired, goggles, gloves, raised coat collar, hat, and sealed arm and trouser ends. There was not the protective clothing available today, these lousily paid labourers depended on cast-off overalls and jackets supplied to enginemen, caps, too.

The tubing equipment consisted of stout flexible hose with fixed small bore metal tube. This was attached to compressed air supply valves located at various points throughout the shed and served by a chattering Westinghouse steam pump close to the stationary boiler. The long metal stem on the air hose was inserted into each and every tube and dirt attacked with a shot of compressed air controlled by brass hand trigger. If these blasts didn't clear the tubes a long metal rod and physical force were applied. In the cab and firebox there was a thick coating of soot which only a water hose could shift.

This work was usually done after a boiler had been washed out. It was also an opportunity to replace oil trimmings. These worsted syphons were made by two old drivers with seats by the fire in the oil store. There were various types of trimmings including plug, plug tail, "T" tail and pad. The plug tail trimming was used in oil boxes and fed oil to axle boxes, slide bars, horn cheeks, etc. A simple plug trimming was used in big ends where movement threw oil over the plug and allowed this lubricant to drop on the crank. A "T" tail trimming syphoned oil from a box and down a pipe into fixed parts of the locomotive. Pad trimmings came ready made and were chiefly used in underkeeps of axle boxes. The worsted pad on a wide spring is supplied with oil by tail feeders attached to the pad and dipping into a bath of oil in the underkeeps. The spring body allowed for compression under the axle end. Making trimmings was skilled work and ideal for young drivers with a bent for learning. This opportunity arose when the regular men were on rest day or holidays.

In the oil store there were also boiler gauge glasses of various sizes to suit particular locomotives. In the same drawer there was a supply of corks for oil ways on engine motions. These corks had a hollow cane inside to allow for air to enter oilways and avoid air locks.

I once had a neighbour who was a salesman for a cork manufacturer and I told him to approach the railway stores people in Glasgow for an order. He didn't quite understand why steam engines needed corks but I explained the reason and told him corks with canes through them were preferable. This neighbour, an old school pal of mine, got in touch with Glasgow and won a big order for corks fitted with canes.

In an emergency a driver would plug an oilway with cotton waste or an ordinary bottle cork. It was not unusual to see locomotives adorned with whisky bottle corks and because of their wide tops they were easy to handle but there was always the danger of air locks in the oil way.

A driver on engine preparation work carried a horse-shoe nail to remove stubborn corks and one could often hear the cry "has some b..... put this in with a hammer?" Oiling steam engines was a dirty business but one dressed accordingly and also carried a sack or waterproof sheet to lie on while oiling a Stephenson link gear. As the oiler reached down into the bowels of the engine on a wet day water could run off the boiler and on to his back. As I say, he would be dressed for the occasion so the preparation man was happy as water dripped from his nose, he couldn't get any wetter.

Correct setting was important when oiling below a Gresley three cylinder loco, the centre big end should preferably be on the bottom front quarter, not always possible if engine was buffered up to others as was usual in St Margarets. When there was room for movement, however, the driver would watch the left big end as the fireman moved the loco after preliminary warning. Setting was right when the left big end stopped on the bottom front angle this meant the centre big end was near its lowest point and convenient for oiling from the pit bottom, although the driver was placed between ashpan and big end. One had to remind the fireman not to disturb the fire and send hot ashes on to his mate below. A setting from the right side of a Gresley three cylinder loco could be judged by the position of the eccentric arm which matched the setting of the centre big end.

Chapter 5

Well Oiled

Class 'A2' Thompson and Peppercorn locos had inside motions less convenient than Gresley engines. It was difficult to reach the centre small end on an "A2" and a driver had to be something of a contortionist to climb up from the pit. I saw a Dundee driver overcome this problem one day by holding the legs of his agile mate as this worthy hung low under the boiler with oil pourie directed at small end cups.

The NE Class J50's known as 'submarines' because of their smokebox hugging side tanks were practically inaccessible to an oiler. The narrow aperture at the bottom of sloping tank seemed to say "oil me if you dare". The oiler was obliged to go below to reach the gearing and even in daylight a flare lamp was necessary to overcome the darkness caused by the ugly tank extension. This was not one of Gresley's better designs.

A greasers' job in St Margarets was a dirty business in every way but if you got on with your work and co-operated with the gaffer nobody bothered you. Some-times, a train driver would pay a greaser to prepare his engine every day, it was worth it to come on duty clean and tidy and simply step on to the engine and away.

Apart from oiling by hand there were also mechanical lubricators and hydrostatic sight feed lubricators to replenish. The driver dealt with the mechanical lubrication while the fireman seen to the hydrostatic type. When the Westinghouse pump was fitted to engines it was the fireman's job to fill the oil cup on these.

An engine from the works after overhaul usually had

mechanical lubricators on full feed. Such lubricators consisted of a cast-iron box into which was fitted a number of independent oil pumps, all of which operated simultaneously. The box itself formed an oil container and was fitted with a hinged lid for the purpose of replenishing the oil which was filtered through a fine-mesh sieve. The supply pumps were double acting, oil being delivered on both the up and down movements giving a continuous oil supply. The lubricator was driven from some convenient point on the motion through a ratchet which drove the shaft in one direction. On each end of the shaft was a cam working in slots on the driving frame, the latter being so arranged to slide vertically in guide at each end of lubricating box. When the driving shaft revolved a reciprocating motion was given to the frame which was connected to the pump plunger by means of thimbles.

These lubricators could be in the cab or outside on the footplate and dispensed cylinder oil as well as engine oil. High up on the footplate of a Pacific Class loco there was little room to replenish a mechanical lubricator but usually on inspection the pumps were covered with oil, enough to satisfy requirements. An engine newly from the shops and smelling of hot fresh paint would be suspect and on opening the lubricator lid the pumps could be clearly seen with only a film of oil to cover their nakedness. This meant at least eight pints of oil over and above specific requirements and to obtain extra oil at St Margarets a driver had to ask the gaffer for a chit. This was a mere formality but when the chit was presented at the oil store the storeman would have a grouse — "What are you doing with the b..... stuff — drinking it!?" Eight pints poured into an empty mechanical lubricator barely covered the pumps.

The Reid designed Class J37 loco of NBR origin had a mechanical lubricator on the outside footplate delivering cylinder oil to the front. This treacle-like lubricant tended to solidify in cold weather and to guard against this it was steam heated through narrow copper pipes lying along the footplate. This is where a driver had to lie to reach the driving shaft for oiling purposes — fitters, too, doing a repair. Not surprisingly, there were howls of pain when the forgetful gent came in contact with those hot pipes. The cry would be "oh you b......!" and someone passing would say "who's a b......?!"

Chapter 6

Steam Engine Fitter

A steam fitter's job in St Margarets was no less grim than that of a driver greaser. Looking back now it seems an unreal world. I know a fitter whose body was permanently bent. He had been examining an engine stopped for boiler washing and when he was in the examination pit the blow down cock was opened. Only those who have seen this terrific blast can appreciate the horror of the situation. But the fitter survived and later continued his examining career — he didn't have to bend far, thereafter.

Brake block fitting was an unenviable task and St Margarets had a full time "blocker" whose mate kept him supplied with brake blocks. People doing such work on a regular basis soon became adept but ask a man to block an engine occasionally and he'll shrink or quail through fear. Adjusting or shifting a brake is more simple and fitters would smile at a repair card reading "brake to shift" or "brake to adjust" but if the fitter read "engine to block" the work would be targeted on the expert blocker.

Brake gearings were of two designs; a rod with fork end and holes to engage a securing pin; and a rod threaded to allow a big nut to tighten the gearing.

The vacuum automatic brake had specialist treatment in St Margarets and a fitter was fully employed with vacuum troubles. Although outside his regular daytime working hours any fitter could be called to deal with a defect in the vacuum system. During the day Tommy Houliston was the vacuum king.

Some small Class Y9 dock pugs had only a handbrake and No 68119 was the St Margarets 'pet'. Drivers with nothing else to do would put in a repair card for No 68119 reading 'vacuum to test' or 'engine to jack up under whistle'. The fitter who collected such a card would walk away dreamily then suddenly stop in his stride as he realised the joke was on him.

Willie Paterson was a fitter who specialised in lubricators and when he was on duty during the day a driver would go direct to Willie with any lubrication problems. Willie was also a first aid man and looked after the ambulance room at the foot of the main shed. He also attended football matches and other public events in his capacity as a St Andrews Ambulance First-aider. Other fitters in St Margarets also participated in this work.

I was glad of such a person on the occasion when I was climbing down from the cab of a Class J83 engine and was struck on the head by a lump of coal. This engine had a narrow bunker and most of the coal being tipped landed on the cab roof and the ground. The tipper should have given me time to get clear after setting engine at tip but I spent the rest of my night shift in Edinburgh Royal Infirmary having my head wound stitched, escorted by the fitter first aid man.

An engineman could learn a lot by watching fitters at work, that's how I discovered all the 'mysteries' inside the dome atop the boiler. When doing dome work the fitter would arrange for the engine to be set below a rafter in the shed roof then, using a long ladder, would attach block and tackle to the rafter and use this gear to remove dome cover. Looking into this housing I could see the steam regulator main valve, regulator pilot valve, regulator head and injector steam pipe, names that were less meaningful in the classroom. It was a simple matter to picture the steam events in the dome later when I was driving.

Other interesting work could be seen in the fitting shops at the foot of the long shed. There was the wheel drop where wheels were removed and turned on a lathe to re-align tyres and flanges. The latter, when too sharp, could cause a derailment by splitting points. Thats the first thing checked when engine or vehicles are derailed; the gauge of rails is also measured.

Axle boxes are re-metalled in the fitting shop. The built-in recesses in the curved brass parts are filled with molten white metal. When hard this metal melts at a comparatively low temperature when exposed to friction and controls damage to bearings. In practice a 'hot box' as it is called can be smelt and a hot centre big end on a Gresley engine smells strongly of garlic when heat causes a small container to burst. The boiler bottom is usually splattered with white metal and the smell of garlic persists long after the event.

Chapter 7

Environmentally Friendly St Margarets

When I went to St Margarets in the summer of 1936 it looked a forbidding place, much more ugly than Haymarket and ecologically inferior to the Gresley showroom I had forsaken for promotion. At that time 64B was a glamour shed, a charm school for 'enginemen elite' and didn't deserve to be alphabetically behind 64A, in fact, this LMS system of identification hadn't yet arrived. Who would want to leave express passenger engines and get involved with run down goods engines? Both places had large cleaning squads but there wasn't the same satisfaction in cleaning an ancient goods engine rather than a brand new Class P2 or A4 and A3. Admittedly, St Margarets had handsome NB Atlantics and Scotts in abundance with romantic names but at Haymarket there was an atmosphere of adventure, the start of a new era in railway history and less black reek.

In that 'smoke chamber' misleadingly called St Margarets however, I found a camaraderie unmatched. Looking back now I think this sociality was founded on adversity, we were all in the same stinking mess. Whatever it was, it was a great feeling to belong to such a caring fraternity.

We had cleaning squads on every shift and in between shifts, the latter being called 'flying squads'. These were made up of men qualified for firing duties, 'passed cleaners' they were called. Should the running foreman require a fireman in a hurry he called on the senior man in the 'flying squad'. Actually the senior man tried to keep in sight of the running office so the foreman didn't have far to call.

The youngest cleaners in the main squads worked on the inside gearings, very dirty work. Then in order of seniority there were two men on the wheels at each side, one on the 'paintwork' the name given to the short skirt below footplate, also buffer beam and cab sides. There were two men on the boiler, one on each side, and one man cleaned the whole smokebox. Three men cleaned the tender; one on each side and one at the back.

Certain individuals were responsible for looking after protection boards and scotches, each man had his own cleaning rags (a dozen) and men on the wheels carried buckets of paraffin while boiler cleaners used a white oil based mixture we called "Micky".

We sang and argued as we worked and two men on the tenders lagged behind as they argued more seriously on subjects such as "Is marriage legal prostitution?"

Donald Whyte was our gaffer and was minus his left arm and right leg. This happened when he was about 18 and was knocked down by a Class J36 0-6-0 engine. Every time he passed this loco he gave it a whack with his stick. Despite his serious disability Donald was a working gaffer and would rub at an engine with his right hand while his left stump moved in unison.

As a Border man he was keen on rugby and we took advantage of this by getting him talking about the game and forgetting work. Then he would suddenly realise our ruse and call out 'Right lads, next engine, No 9434 — a wash all over'.

When Donald lit his pipe he would hold the matchbox between his knees and strike a match with this right hand, puffing the pipe with his head near the matchbox. He carried cotton waste in his right coat pocket and used this to wipe his one hand, this made his coat very shiny with oil but he kept his independence. I only saw him beaten once, it was winter time, roads thick with ice and Donald had a struggle to get home in the morning. That night he came to work with both feet wrapped in sacking to grip the ice. The squad made sure he had no trouble after that, we carried him home.

St Margarets first A3 Pacific loco arrived on the scene in 1937, it was No 2752 "Spion Kop", named after the 1920 Derby winner, the year I was born. This engine was used to work the 1210 pm Pullman ex Waverley to Carlisle returning with the 6.29 pm ex Carlisle, a top link job. We didn't only clean this engine we burnished the front buffers and smokebox hinges. Then when the train was due to pass through St Margarets heading for the Waverley Route Donald had us lined up to cheer Spion Kop on its way.

Sunday night was the worst time in St Margarets when engines were kindled and the reek thick. It was impossible to work in the shed and cleaners and others found work outside until the smoke cleared, or at least some of it. There were never clear skies above St Margarets.

After booking on duty at a time office close to the access road named Clockmill Road enginemen would proceed up a slight slope to the bothies, one for drivers and fireman the other for cleaners. These places looked like massive barns with whitewashed walls, but were in fact the original machine shops dating back to 1846 when St Margarets was the first NBR engine works. Lathe supports were still embedded in thick stone walls and the high ceiling black and covered with years of oil and dirt blended with the darkness. Two feeble light bulbs were in constant use because daylight never penetrated this dungeon-like accommodation. Two long tables with metal tops stood on one side with black wooden benches affording convenient seating. In the middle of the floor a coal stove burned fiercely or stood dead according to the weather. At the far end there was a cold water tap dripping onto an ugly sink and close to a brick window-sill worn down by men rubbing their hands on the bricks to remove dirt after a soft soap application.

As some cleaners sat talking others played cards — pontoon. Then the peace was disturbed as the door was thrown open and a gruff voice shouted "right lads — across the road!" the order to proceed to the engine shed. But first, the cleaners had to collect cleaning material and lamps from the tool-store. There was much banter and hilarity before this column of workers headed for the workplace. A double main line had to be crossed and on the night shift this usually coincided with the passing of the Coronation express. As we stood at the crossing where indicators told us "Down train approaching" we would hear the drone of an A4 whistle then feel the blast as the Coronation sped on its way to Waverley station, the end of its 6½ hour journey from Kings Cross.

This was followed by a great influx of engines, those that had been queuing outside waiting for the Coronation to clear. Some shysters wished these engines would follow the A4 to Haymarket. Even if they did there was still more than enough work in St Margarets for cleaners.

These able young lads were also handy for last minute replacements if certain workers failed to appear for duty. The trade union might frown on such versatility but the extra pay was attractive to a cleaner laddie who in those days earned only a morsel — about 24 shillings a week — £1.20p.

I found myself looking after a sand kiln more than once. This involved shovelling wet sand on to a fixed sieve where it was heated and dried before permeating into hoppers. Firemen requiring sand for their engines would bring a bucket to the hopper, pull up a small shutter and allow hot dry sand to fill the bucket, red hot like cinders.

Cleaners could also substitute for firedroppers but ashpan work was frowned on because of danger to eyesight which was very important to a man in the line of promotion. In pre war days engine fires were cleaned outside No 1 and No 6 roads in the main shed and disposal enginemen did this work. During the war the roundhouse known as the NE shed because it once housed NE engines was demolished and straight disposal lyes installed along with a 70 ft turntable.

Gland packing was another job undertaken by cleaners and St Margarets had plenty engines using soft packing, the Class J's for instance. The gland packer's equipment included sacking to lie on, asbestos packing, a gland key and a lamp. After consulting the repair book and finding an engine needing glands packed the gland packer would go to this engine and place "not to be moved boards" on lamp brackets back and front then advise the running foreman of the situation. If the gaffer required a shunt this was done before the glandpacker settled down to his task.

Asbestos packing came in small rolls and was impregnated with grease, flexible and limp, its thickness depending on its use. The experienced glandpacker knew the length of packing required for a particular engine and this length would be cut from the roll then hammered flat against the footplate. Gland nuts had to be loosened to allow sleeve to be drawn back giving access for new packing after removal of old packing. Once the new packing had been stuffed into the stuffing box the sleeve was tightened up against the new packing, hopefully making the piston way steam tight. The driver would appreciate this repair because St Margarets engines did a lot of shunting and steam blowing from pistons hid his view of the shunters' signals.

Labouring work with higher pay also attracted engine cleaners, shovelling coal on the coal stage or cleaning pits on shed, mate to a fitter or mate to a boilersmith. If the pay was right the job was right for ever-eager youths with plenty of uses for money.

During my early years at St Margarets there were no staff amenities, no encouragement to teach or learn. The Mutual Improvement Class (MIC) had to make do with an ancient NBR carriage body for a classroom. Staunch members of the MIC kept this hovel clean and tutored others aiming to become engine drivers. Workers organised their own social activities in a wooden hut overlooking the gloom that was St Margarets. Hard labour may have weakened the flesh but the spirit was strong. This immaterial part of man created the St Margarets Pipe Band and every week drivers, firemen, cleaners and artisan workers practised outside the carriage shops on the north side of the depot. Depending on their call to duty some men wore their Highland dress while others appeared in overalls but all were armed with the all important pipes and drums. Workers on duty were given an impromptu performance of pipe band music, marching and counter-marching. People passing in trains and seeing such a sight must have wondered what was being celebrated.

St Margarets also had a football team in the amateur league managed by Driver Bob Wright who also acted running foreman at times.

There was no National Health Service so conditions were right to nurture sick funds and St Margarets had two benevolent assets — the "Abbey Fund" and the "Forty Thieves". Volunteers collected contributions on pay day so, on leaving the pay queue a man would pay his Trade Union's due then the Abbey and/or Forty Thieves. The beauty of these funds was that, irrespective of any claims for sick benefit, there was a disbursement of funds at Christmas — enough for a few drinks and a bottle of whisky for New Year time.

Pay day was an opportunity to renew friendships after losing touch when working on different shifts. You would see how friends looked in a dress suit after having known someone only in railway uniform. It was also an occasion to meet retired men and go for a drink in a local pub or the railway club and talk about past experiences on the job. There was a unique opportunity amongst railwaymen possibly because no other job could compare. What other worker has booking on times like 11.59 pm, 1.46 am, 4.12 am, and so on, their whole life geared to trains and timetables with the temperamental steam locomotive as an anchor?

This all but human machine could influence a man's character, his peculiar distinctive qualities or traits. Enginemen usually had a long affair with the steam engine, a lifetimes' marriage, if there were rails to their home they would take the thing home with them. It wasn't railway property, it was Tom Smith's engine or some other regular driver.

*1. Class A3 No 60086 "Gainsborough" (Leeds) heads
express passenger train in Glasgow.   (A A McLean)*

*2. St Margarets 0-6-0 Class J37 No 64576 heads a local
passenger train at Dunbar – cleaned for
the occasion too! (A A McLean)*

3. *Thornton 0-6-0 Class J37 No 64570 hauls a coal train past Thornton Weighs. The signalman in the picture was proud of having worked in the same box for 50 years.*

4. *The Thornton Breakdown Crane was used at one time for lifting locos to release wheels and axle boxes for repair. Installation of a wheel drop in the Fitting Shop dispensed with this crane work.*

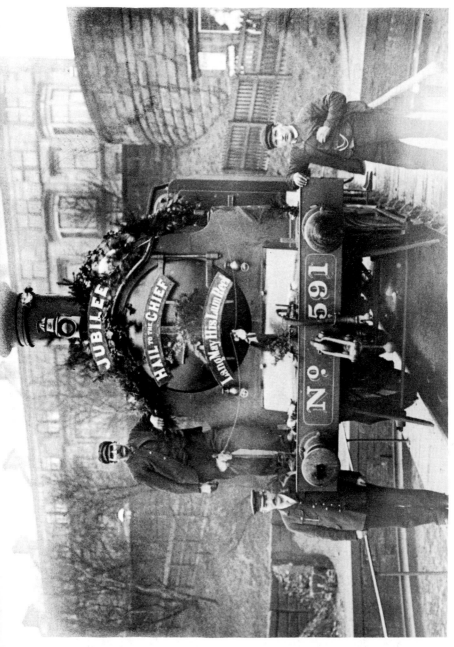

5. NBR 0-4-4 tank engine No 591 was allocated to Kipps (Coatbridge) and worked suburban passenger trains between Hamilton and Hyndland. Train crew uniforms and youthful appearance of the driver (right) are of particular interest, as is the decorated loco. (D Crichton)

6. Class D49 No 62708 "Argyllshire" pulls away from Leuchars Junction with an express passenger train. The station pilot, a class B1, can be seen in the background.

7. LNER Pacific No 2566 "Ladas" (BR No 60067) at Glasgow (Queen Street) not far from its North British Locomotive works birthplace. These right-hand drive engines were more suited to the North Eastern Region for signal sighting.

8. *0-6-0T 2F Class J83 No 68353 shunting at Thornton depot with Driver James Ritchie. Slack couplings and solid buffers were a recipe for rough shunting.*

9. *Class A4 No 60009 "Union of South Africa" with the Royal Highlander in Royal Highland surroundings. Scotland's fastest steam locomotive beside Scotland's fastest river (the Spey) near Newtonmore. This is the engine Driver James Paterson had for 12 years and "loved like a woman".*

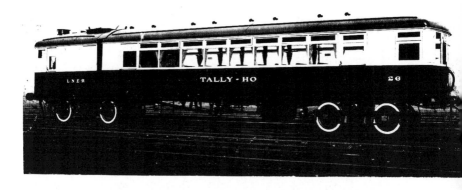

10. *100hp Sentinel No 26 "Tally-Ho" at York, in March 1928. Note the chimney has a spark arresting device. These steam coaches were named after stage coaches and there was a framed history of each stage coach inside.*

11. *St Margaret's Pipe Band (1933) ready for a "blow-up" of a different kind to that experienced with steam engines. In the background is a J Holmes GER 0-6-0ST. Several classes were built, none of which had any claim to beauty. The carriage shops, of NBR origin are in the far background and the tall stack of a stationary boiler can be seen to the right.*
Band rehearsal was in the evening when carriage repair work had ceased. Note the LNER uniform hats, unlike the LMS and BR they had leather chin straps and were without oil-proof tops. (M Brown)

12. St Margaret's freight locos in Craigentinny Loop. These engines were dispersed from the main depot at weekends to combat smoke nuisance. (Rae Montgomery)

13. The well-known D30 Scott Class "Wandering Willie" at Hawick.

14. *Class Y9 pugs at St Margarets adjacent to the water tank
(5,400 gallons) and sand kiln. Note the snow plough on the
ground and man up telegraph pole.*
(H C Casserley)

15. *Class V2 No 60812 at Morningside Road with empty
coaches en route to Waverley station to work a passenger
train south. Circumambience, no doubt, but operationally
convenient. (A A McLean)*

Chapter 8

Pushing up Daisies

In pre-war days men nursed their machines; they cleaned and polished inside and outside and would remove oil trimmings to save wastage while the engine was stabled. After the war when massive deterioration had set in and maintenance neglected, St Margarets' engines became a joke. I remember firing Glen Garry, an ex NBR 4-4-0, in 1947 and having had the same engine for nearly a week I cleaned the boiler faceplate and made it shine with some cylinder oil. As we ran through Edinburgh's eastern suburbs en route to Hawick I gave the faceplate a wee rub as I stood in the well of the cab. My driver then leaned towards me as Glen Gerry clattered on its way and, pointing to a local cemetery, he said "you're wasting your time, Charlie, men who fussed over this engine years ago are pushing up daisies over there". His remarks did nothing to dishearten me but I found myself wishing I had been around when enginemen took a pride in their engines. I was just a cleaner laddie but I can remember when firemen lifted the floorboards and hosed the dirt away underneath. Some of these conscientious men even carried wee paint brushes to clean behind boiler gauge glass columns and other faceplate fittings.

Watering facilities in St Margarets were totally inadequate and designed for small engines. When shed roads were full, as they often were, a large engine couldn't get near the water column unless facing west with water tank near the column. The usual procedure was to fill the tank of a big engine then "stick it" on the end of a road as they used to say. In that way badly needed space was utilized.

Sometimes a tank would overflow when the driver was away from the water handle and the fireman doing something else. The cascading water would run into the pit and maybe drain away if the drain was not blocked with ashes. If the drain was blocked the water would collect in the examination pit and men working below other engines would soon find themselves ankle deep in water.

The running shed was quite unsuitable for examining engines especially if the engine was being stopped for boiler washing, an opportunity to do extensive repairs. During the '50s it was decided to construct a new examination pit with fluorescent lighting to help the examiner to spot defects. This new pit was sited well away from the centre of activity, at the end of what was known as the crane road, a road used for storing dead locos awaiting repair. Consequently a great deal of space was sacrificed in keeping access open to this fine new facility. As was expected this access soon became obstructed as old habits returned and a bright new concrete pit with inbuilt strip lighting lay black and buried under dead engines. The planners had no idea of conditions in St Margarets and tended to design useless innovations which, theoretically, seemed fine.

The mechanical foreman had overall responsibility for the condition of locomotives and kept records of their state of repair. Eventually, a "shopping proposal" would be necessary because of continuing deterioration of an engine's structure. The Chief Mechanical Engineer (CME) would then arrange for the engine to be shopped. Understandably this didn't happen immediately it was a long process. Meanwhile, the engine would be withdrawn from traffic and laid aside in the ever present line-up of dead engines. Eventually word would be received to send the engine to the works. Cowlairs, Inverurie or Doncaster.

It could be an intermediate repair or a general repair according to mileage and other factors. Sometimes the engine was able to work a train to a particular area or travel light but more often the loco was hauled dead. I remember taking duty on a winter's night at 9 o'clock as a "spare" driver. "Ah!" said the Running Foreman, "I've got a nice job for you tonight, Charlie, away over to No 7 road there's a big Green Arrow for Cowlairs Works. I want you to caretake that engine. "I'll give the 10 o'clock man a B1 to haul you to Eastfield".

There is nothing colder than cold steel and when I climbed into the cab of the Green Arrow I thought, "What have I done to deserve this"? As I stood there with coat collar high and hands in pockets I shivered at the prospect of riding in this ice-box surrounded by rusting steel and minus storm sheet protection.

In a situation like this it was usual to hoist a brazier aboard and get a fire going. I had just got this fire going when the B1 backed on to my engine and the fireman shouted "Are ye awright, Charlie?" as he prepared to couple on. "Awright?" I said, "I'll never be awright after this lot!"

As we got underway a cold wind blew the smoke from the brazier into my face, a kind of hell in the Antarctic. There were 28 signal boxes between St Margarets and Cowlairs junction and we were shunted at every one. As soon as the wheels stopped turning I raced forward to the B1 for a heat and a hot drink. I was never so glad to leave an engine as I was that cold morning at Eastfield.

Almost immediately I climbed up on a real engine ready to leave the shed to work the newspaper train from Queen Street station to Waverley. I alighted at Queen Street platform and found a cosy corner on the paper train where I slept throughout the journey to Edinburgh and home.

An intermediate repair at the works was literally a patched up job. Engines having had this kind of repair were easily recognised by welded patches on boiler, tender or elsewhere with a dab of black paint to further show where rotting metal had been reinforced. A general repair brought forth a new engine freshly painted all over. Engines from Inverurie Works were sent to Ferryhill steam depot for running in and might be found anywhere on the former Great North of Scotland Railway (GNSR) system. Locomotives out of Cowlairs Works were "run in" at

Eastfield and could work on the West Highland line. Sometimes Eastfield had the audacity to book these engines on Edinburgh jobs and they could be seen passing through St Margarets. It was then the gaffer would hurry to the phone and alert the Control and maybe arrange a change-over. Occasionally a driver or fireman in conversation with a gaffer would mention having seen a St Margarets engine ex works in a place it should never have been. This would start proceedings to get the 'lost' loco back to St Margarets. When the wanderer did return it was automatically stopped for boiler washing.

I remember having a Class J36 No 65224 on a job and as I stood waiting to leave shed I thought this engine, new out of the works, should have a name. I consulted my Ian Allan ABC book and sure enough the engine was "Mons". On my return to shed I booked a few small jobs and wrote "engine to name". Next day when I saw this engine the name "Mons" had been painted in yellow on each driving splasher, not by a signwriter but by an ordinary craftsman who cared.

Chapter 9

A Not So Happy New Year

New Year in Scotland is an important celebration, an extended holiday. Hogmanay was like the usual Saturday night at St Margarets. As the engines came through the coal store most of them were marked "all fire out" (AFO). In fact it was easier to tell the firedroppers what fires had to be kept going. Men were keen to get finished work and join the festivities and the arrangement adopted called for an all out effort before midnight and the new year. There were usually enough "abstainers" on duty who volunteered to keep a clear head and look after engines in steam. Those people keen to celebrate were not discouraged and could 'disappear' after midnight. The danger in accommodating these revellers was clearly seen one hogmanay Saturday at Portobello when I worked on the shunting engines there.

A driver agreed to his fireman's request to go "first footing" and this eager young man set off to visit friends and relatives as they celebrated the New Year. Other enginemen at Portobello were quite happy to relax and have an early finish. After drawing the engine fires and securing these engines we all went home to a more congenial New Year atmosphere — bed!

The driver whose mate had gone celebrating was rudely awakened by a banging on his door about 8 o'clock that Sunday morning. It was the police who informed him his fireman had been badly injured at Portobello.

This young man had been crossing the railway yard to rejoin his engine when he was knocked down by a train and severely injured. He managed to haul himself into a brakevan and lie there moaning in agony. A passing guard heard his plaintive cries and investigated then arranged medical attention. The injured fireman lost a leg but after recovery he was accommodated as a level crossing keeper and always had a cheerful wave for St Margarets men who kept him supplied with coal.

Such fateful thoughts were not in the minds of workers at the depot as they hurried to finish work and celebrate New Year. Mechanical noises and hissing steam gave way to a cacophony of sound as engine whistles were tied down and New Year celebrated in style, the noise rising from the bowl housing St Margarets and reverberating from the high tenements above.

"First footing" on the job meant visiting bothies and running office and having a dram in a teacup. A gift of coal was considered to be lucky so there was plenty of coal for this purpose.

The death-like appearance of a place like St Margarets was a sad sight to the enthusiasts and the same sadness prevailed during the 1955 locomans' strike. At that time there was a driver acting assistant running foreman to a man who tried to keep St Margarets alive by shunting engines, stoking fires and filling tanks. The driver assistant went along with this strike-breaking for a start but when he could see no end to it he decided to walk out and join other enginemen.

This strike had its lighter moments and one I remember was when a driver walked into the bothy just before midnight when the strike was due to start. "Some picket that is!" he declared, "they're so busy concentrating on the front entrance the back entrance is unguarded. I walked through the tunnel into the depot without being challenged". On hearing this his attentive audience became restless and threatened to kill him. Just then the gaffer walked in and shouted "Hey, Eddie, you might have left your engine clear of the crossing, there's nobody here to shift it". Eddie had been working empty coaches with a Class V3 and on arrival in shed had left his engine carelessly parked thinking it wouldn't make any difference in a depot on strike. His associates in the bothy thought he was coming *on* duty, not finishing and Eddie's sense of humour urged him to keep them guessing.

St Margarets post war allocation of about 220 engines could not possibly be accommodated in such a small area but at the weekends the impossible was being attempted. Outside roads stretching to within sight of Piershill Junction signalbox were filled with dead engines most of them high capacity Pacifics, Green Arrows and Class K3's. The shed was well filled, every lye solid with engines, likewise the roads behind the shed.

Over on the north side of the main line the ancient roundhouse was overflowing with pugs and lines reserved for carriage and wagon activities were crammed with locos — an engine spotter's delight.

The old roundhouse marked the beginning of the North British Railway Company in 1846 and was really a polygon, rectilinear, of more than four angles and near the general office and blacksmith shop. There was a 42 foot turntable hand pushed with limited clearance of locos stabled there. Access was through a big stone archway on the east side surmounted by a large metal water tank holding 5,400 gallons a mere 'drop in the ocean' when compared with the water tank beside the coalbank with a capacity for 101,950 gallons. Near this entrance there was a sand kiln and water column.

This had been the NBR's only covered accommodation for locomotives during the first twenty-four years of its existence. In 1921 the shed roof was badly damaged by fire and never replaced. The walls were demolished prior to the end of WW 2. The entrance and water tank seemed indestructible and stood like a huge monument to past endeavours. This was where enginemen had to prepare locomotives for work, no protection whatsoever in dreich weather conditions.

Because of the smoke nuisance engines were dispersed to Craigentinny loop every Sunday. These engines, mostly 'J' Class for freight working, were prepared and oil syphons removed. They would leave the depot in convoy, five at a time — the limit for such a movement, with a driver and fireman on leading loco and a driver caretaking in rear. After delivering to Craigentinny a fireman was there to tend the engines and the trainmen returned to St Margarets at a leisurely pace. On one occasion a driver complained about having to walk back and insisted on transport, the liaison van being used to pick him up. "Thats fine with me", said the gaffer, "the quicker you're back the quicker you'll be away again with more engines".

On Monday morning engines at Craigentinny were allocated jobs and when the men took duty they were advised accordingly. Sometimes it was possible to get a lift on a light engine going in that direction or the liaison van. The driver on reaching his loco would replace oil syphons and check the mechanical parts and sand boxes (very important in collieries). The fireman would have to shovel coal forward on the tender and check the water tank and spread fire then the engine would move ahead to South Leith Junction for water before going to starting point for work.

Nearby where these locos were stabled over the weekend there was an oil storage depot built in 1947 when there was a coal shortage and oil burning locomotives were expected to be needed. The crisis passed and the expensive oil depot lay dormant but it gave shelter to the fireman detailed to look after the engines stored in Craigentinny Loop.

Chapter 10

Mind Fill The Boiler

As the big engines were shunted into outside roads at St Margarets on Saturday night the gaffer would remind the enginemen to fill the boilers. When the time came to kindle these engines on Sunday an empty boiler would mean dragging a hose bag to the nearest hydrant, far removed from the empty boiler, a lot of hard and unnecessary work. No wonder gaffers bawled "Mind fill that boiler!"

The locomotive tender, or small compartments on other engines, are the means of fuel and water supplies and although important, of course, they are nothing exciting to look at. The water tank, however, could become troublesome if neglected. Before water is fed to steam injectors and the boiler it passes through roses, perforations in a bulbous fitting inside the tanks similar to a garden watering can. The flow of water can be controlled locally while roses are cleaned. Over a period of time a great deal of sludge collects in a locomotive tank and has to be shovelled out after tank is drained. Sometimes cotton waste or sweat cloth would be accidentally dropped into the tank and would smother the rose(s) and stem the flow of water thus causing an injector failure. On seeing a repair entry reading "roses to examine and clean" a fitter would remove one or both roses and clean the obstruction then blast the rose with water under pressure to further ensure a clear passage.

In a big tank there is room to use a shovel but small tanks are very restricted and very dark. The constant replenishing of water tanks created a stir and prevented undue fouling but dirty roses was one course of injector failure and could not be discounted.

There were strengthening steel beams inside water tanks and when taking on water the flexible leather bag could weigh heavily and bend over an interior beam. From the ground an engineman might not notice anything out of order but a look inside the tank would show the loaded bag bent double and resting on a beam allowing only a trickle of water through. On side tank engines or saddle tanks such a ballooning would cause the bag to explode outwards and drench people in the vicinity.

Careless overflows would rain into axle boxes and displace oil resulting in hot journals. On big tenders there were built in pipes to drain the water to below the tender. If these drain pipes became obstructed by coal spillage overflow would build up at the back of the tender and cascade to the ground. This would be dangerous any-where, but on the main line where quick braking was sometimes necessary such a flood could soak men working on the track and cause injury and panic. In darkness, when water cascades from the back of the tender an engineman might think the tank is full but closer inspection would probably reveal an empty, rusting, iron cavity and a driver about to set out on a long journey would quietly murmur "I'm glad I had a close look".

One St Margarets driver didn't have a closer look. He accepted the engine (a Green Arrow) had been prepared and went to Niddrie to work the 12.30 am express freight to Newcastle. While negotiating the crossover at Monktonhall Junction the V2 was on the boil as the fireman slammed coal into a raging furnace. Suddenly the singing exhaust injector stopped singing and the fireman tried to restart it — but to no avail. He then opened the test cock on the tank but not a drop of water could be seen — the tank was very, very dry. The situation was critical and as the driver viewed the disappearing water level in the boiler and the fierce fire he hoped he could make it to Longniddry and the water supply there but — no chance. He stopped the train at St Germains Level Crossing signalbox and quickly dropped the fire thereby avoiding damage to the fusible plug and firebox. Control was advised and arrangements made to work the train forward and haul the Green Arrow back to St Margarets. All this trouble because the tank hadn't been properly filled.

The average fireman would look upon coal as something that had to be shovelled into the firebox, preferably light and often. A better informed person however would recognise the origins of a particular brand and know at once whether or not his engine was going to steam properly. There was no shortage of coalfields in Britain and steam engine sheds had a supply practically on the doorstep. St Margarets had the Midlothian Coalfield and wagons marked 'LOCO' to deliver this coal. The pits were organised under the title Lothian Coal Company and private traders had their own names on their wagons.

A fireman climbing up on his engine might look at large slabs of coal on the tender and say "Oh, Whitehill" the name of the colliery that produced this coal. It was very hard, and difficult to break, usually in slices, like slates. But it had good heating qualities and what couldn't be broken could be lifted by hand into the firebox.

Anthracite was a non-bituminous coal, burning with intense heat without smoke, and with little flame. This was the produce of Wales and a popular export. It is recommended for miniature steam engines. During the 1950's briquettes shaped like eggs came from Wales to St Margarets and more than 10 years later when tenders were being stripped and prepared for scrapping these eggs were still to be seen hidden under slag.

Anticipating the end of a working day (or night) at St Margarets was a comforting consideration of activity no less intense than the exertion of energy demanded by the nature of the work. There were no facilities for washing, no baths or showers, no hot water. Men concerned with half decent hygiene brought toilet requisites from home, a piece of soap wrapped in a dish cloth or piece of towel, and occasionally, shaving kit.

On the engine the firing shovel was used as a sink with

47

hot water being obtained from the boiler. Sometimes, a bucket could be found if one wanted a good sluice. Towards the end of the shift at St Margarets it was like some kind of ritual to see men stripped to the waist and occasionally completely naked as they got rid of the soot and coal dust that clung to their skin like leeches.

These men didn't finish work at 10 pm, say, they were in the queue waiting to book off at the timekeepers office before the official time. The time-keeper would nod and, looking sullenly over his glasses, would check the faces and number calls of the departing workforce.

The carriage and wagon works had a different system, the men and women there had metal number tags which hung on hooks on a big board. These tags were collected by individuals when taking duty and handed back when leaving work for a meal break or at the end of duty. I mention women because in that army of males there were two females employed at repairing wagon sheets.

At the change of shifts when labour was in a state of flux engines were still leaving and arriving. An engine ready for departure could develop a fault, brake or steam injector trouble. The driver would put in a repair card then impatiently search for a fitter. This is where the "old school" rose to the occasion, there were usually long service men who were in no hurry to leave their beloved steam engines and had a "built in" conscientiousness that geared work to their heart, not the clock. These men weren't thinking of pubs closing and missing a bus or train or working unpaid overtime. St Margarets was their salvation, preserving their moral and emotional system, to a distraught driver looking for a quick repair they were real Samaritans though belonging to St Margarets rather than Samaria.

As a driver booked to leave shed at 9.55 pm with a Class J37 I found myself having trouble with the right injector — a dodgy clack valve. This delivery clack valve was not reseating after use causing continuous blow back at overflow pipe below cab steps — not an uncommon fault on steam engines. Unlike other clack valves located outside on boiler top the Class J37 could be dealt with in the cab.

I was lucky to find Jimmy Milne on the shed and told him of my problem. "I'll be right with you, Charlie" he said, and sure enough he was soon dismantling the troublesome injector, using his cap to protect his hands from the extremely hot metal parts. Sometimes a good thump with a piece of wood (not the coalhammer) would dislodge grit and allow the valve to re-seat but it was reassuring to have Jimmy Milne examine and clean the injector rather than go on thumping all night. A steam blow like this interrupts proper sighting when shunting so I felt more at ease after Jimmy's unpaid overtime.

Sand was an important and expensive commodity at St Margarets. These comminuted fragments of chert came under contract from Burntisland, Fife usually in open wagons. Consequently this sand was soaked and extremely heavy with water. A closed van would have been more appropriate and such vehicles were used at one time. Even a wagon sheet would have afforded protection, but it was easy to sense the attitude that prevailed — "Oh, it's only sand — it's only St Margarets".

At a suitable time this wagon of sand was set in No 6 road adjacent to the sand kiln towering above. Once this wagon was in place the road and access to wheeldrop was virtually closed and much needed space lost.

Two labourers would then climb into the sodden wagon, doff their jackets and start shovelling sand. It was like throwing sand towards the sky while aiming for the floor of the elevated kiln. Then the sand had to be moved from the front to the back to make room for more sand. Not only was the work labour intensive, it was very hard labour.

The sand was then shovelled on to a large sieve for drying and as it dried the sand filtered into hoppers. From here firemen would collect it in buckets and limp across the shed to replenish sand boxes on an engine, 12 or more buckets to fill 4 boxes.

After all this hard work it often happened that a fitter

would appear with instructions to "clear sands" or "sands to be made to work". In the process of doing this job the fitter would empty the engine sand boxes and the sand that once lay sodden in the wagon would now look like Burntisland beach with the tide receding in the examination pit. Usually, the cause of "sands not working" was water running off the boiler into the sand boxes resulting in sand clogging the pipes. Had sand boxes been put on top of the boiler as in America and other countries this problem and waste would not have existed.

During its 150 years existence little changed in St Margarets. Right to the end men were struggling to lift heavy leather bags (frozen in winter) into water tanks and awkwardly placed because of congestion. There should have been a large diameter pipe astride the roads with bags that could be controlled at tender level. This would have allowed the driver to get on with his work instead of standing impatiently awaiting to turn off the water when the fireman shouted "right, tank's full!".

As a cleaner I found cleaning wheels and gearing with paraffin was a filthy job and wondered why they didn't use a jet of hot water to shift the muck. Now I see that's exactly what happens in China. Boiler washers had hot water on tap — why not use the same supply for cleaning wheels and gearing?

There were so many obvious improvements which could have been made at St Margarets but LNER money was at that time being channelled into Gresley innovations and publicity for a 'Square Deal' to counteract road competition.

Chapter 11

Enter the "Cammel Car"

The advent and convenience of buses after World War 1 was a contributory factor influencing the introduction of steam railcars. This was not a new idea. In Edwardian England the London and North Western Railway had an 0-4-0 tank engine with inside cylinders totally enclosed in a coach body to which it was articulated. The motion was very violent at any speed and the enclosure of the engine, with connecting doors through the luggage compartment made the coach uncomfortably hot in summer time.

The Great North of Scotland Railway had a rail-motor, as they were called, built by Andrew Barclay, Kilmarnock one of two such contraptions. The design incorporated a Cochran boiler, normally used for stationary engines. The engine was a single driver, the driving wheels leading, this was not a success.

In 1927 the London & North Eastern Railway introduced steam railcars for their branch lines and there was such a vehicle on the Dalmeny-Ratho branch. As a boy at Dalmeny my pals and I used to ask the fireman for "a pennyworth of chips", to our young minds it seemed just like a mobile chip van. Little did I think I would be firing the thing in 1947.

This steam coach was fitted with a Sentinel engine which had given very good service in heavy road haulage until heavy taxation finished it off. The LNER steam coaches had green and cream livery and every car had a name; Flower of Yarrow, Pearl, Royal Eagle, Nettle, Retaliator, to name but a few. One of the last to be withdrawn was Quicksilver named after a stage coach that operated in the

Berwick area. They were all named after stage coaches.

The seating accommodation seemed spacious but it could very soon fill up and overflow on a market day, for instance, or Saturday night out of Glasgow. There was also a big luggage compartment and the coach could be driven from either end — the boiler compartment or driver only end.

In St Margarets the steam coach was housed with locomotives and was subject to the pollution from these. There was also damage to upholstery caused by workers using the coach as a dormitory. So, it was decided to stable Quicksilver at Leith Central station the huge under-used terminal on the suburban railway.

On the day shift my mate and I booked on at 4.30 am at St Margarets and were allowed half-an hour to walk to Leith Central. I used fire-lighters or paraffin soaked waste to light the fire and steam soon registered on the gauge as the small vertical boiler got to work, "Light and often" is the maxim for firing the steam engine but on the Sentinel car it was "light and not so often". The aim was to get a cone shaped fire and three small shovelfuls (kitchen size) at a time was the recommended feed.

We ran light to Longniddry to work a 7.23 am passenger train to Edinburgh (Waverley) and the sprint through East Lothian's fertile fields was an opportunity to get Quicksilver on the boil. As we stood at Longniddry waiting for Haddington connections my driver, Jock McIntosh would go on the scrounge and return with strawberries and fresh farm produce. I couldn't leave Quicksilver unattended, boiler level dropped noticeably and the fire had to be nursed.

Once underway the steam coach responded to the clear country air and miles of flat permanent way more used to Gresley Pacifics and East Coast express trains. The tricky part was yet to come, the steep climb from St Margarets through the Calton Tunnel to Waverley. To the observer Quicksilver lived up to its name with a mercurial run through St Margarets but on the hills the effort was too much for the wee Sentinel engine and thankfully blackness enveloped the steam car's struggle through the tunnel.

On the long, flat run from Longniddry the water level in the boiler had been maintained by an automatic injector geared to the running wheels. Outside the Calton Tunnel, however, and approaching the brow of the hill and level ground in No 2 platform the small conventional injector was in use. Standing on my toes and looking into the water gauge column I could see only the shadow of water as it bobbed in the glass. Then my driver would shut off steam and Quicksilver would glide to a halt at the platform. Neither my mate nor the passengers were aware of my ordeal in the Calton Tunnel and the blessed relief felt when the gauge glass filled with water. There was certainly no chance of steam rocketing to the station roof as was common with conventional steam locomotives. With Quicksilver it was black reek that hit the roof.

I was sitting at Waverley one day preparing for a 12 noon dash to North Leith and coaxing steam into Quicksilver, black smoke like an atomic mushroom near the roof. I could see the locomotive inspector on a distant platform and I seemed to feel his piercing eyes as he glowered in my direction. Next minute he was racing across the concourse and I knew why, he was also known as the "black smoke inspector". As he puffed towards Quicksilver I quickly removed the fire-lid and the black smoke disappeared, then I folded my arms and sat back. "That's better" said the breathless inspector as he closed in on me, and I looked at him as if to say "What are you talking about"?

The run to Leith Citadel station at sea level was mostly down hill. Again, my driver would go on the scrounge and bring to me a huge parcel of fish. When we stopped at Easter Road station en route to Waverley my wife would be there with my 'piece' and I would hand over the fish. As this transaction took place Jock McIntosh, alone at the front, would have a huge grin on his face, happy to see we were happy.

Sometimes, Quicksilver would haul a van of fish to

Waverley and I found she steamed better with this load behind.

The steam coach was known as the Camel car at St Margarets and was allocated special coal. We used to go to Haymarket for this small coal supplied in sacks and delivered through the roof into a hopper adjacent to the boiler. After Quicksilver had been positioned near raised ground (the former coal bank before a mechanical plant was installed) we put a plank across to walk on. As I was humping this coal one day trying to keep my balance, my watchful mate said, "You remind me of a coalman delivering coal to a sixth floor tenement flat, as he made to open the house door he looked back and found he had his horse by the ears". This humour caused me to laugh and I dropped the sack of coal and jumped to the ground. "I won't tell you any more jokes", said Jock McIntosh, "we'll be here all day at this rate".

On arrival at Waverley station "Quicksilver" sometimes ran into No 7 platform at the east end immediately behind Menzies bookstall. As soon as we stopped the bookstall girl, Evelyn Macdonaled used to bring me a cup of tea and a cake, walking past Jock McIntosh in the process. As Jock leaned from his cab eyeing us wonderingly one day he called to Evelyn "What has he got that I haven't got". With flashing eyes Evelyn replied "A cup of tea and a cake", and my mate's mouth fell open speechless.

The fireman on the opposite shift had a less cheerful life with a mate whose disposition showed no gladness or joy, he was selfish and self centred and cared only for his deck chair hire business at Portobello beach. On pay day he would take time off during a quiet spell at Waverley and hurry to St Margarets for his pay, this saved time at the end of his shift when he was relieved at Abbeyhill station. On his return to Waverley he never relieved his fireman to let him get his pay.

He did reluctantly on one occasion when a 'spare' fireman was on the job. This man knew about the driver's selfishness and set about teaching the deck chair man a lesson. When the driver had collected his pay at St Margarets he returned to Quicksilver and made himself comfortable. "Right" said the 'spare' fireman, "I'm away for my pay, I won't be long", and off he went.

Instead of returning to Quicksilver the 'spare' fireman sat in a compartment of a train in an adjacent platform watching the driver's antics. As the minute hand of the big station clock jerked its way around the face moving ever closer to 12 noon starting time the driver checked it with his own watch and was near panic stricken as he looked in vain for his fireman. With barely a minute to spare the fireman stepped from his hidey-hole across into the cab of Quicksilver. At this point the guard was walking towards the demented driver waving a green flag and blowing hard on his whistle. Just as he felt he had some explaining to do the driver caught a glimpse of his mate busy in the cab of the steam coach. "Where have you been!?" he demanded of his fireman. "Me?" said the innocent looking stoker, "I've been away for my pay". The driver had no answer for this and ever after the fireman on the job went for his pay like the driver.

Chapter 12

Vegetables and VIPs

A shift foarit (forward) at St Margarets brought joyful anticipation amongst young enginemen. This came at the start of the holiday period when the number of men in a link was increased. In summer time the "big spare" link had 52 different shifts (one for each week of the year) to cover every eventuality. The increase in passenger traffic affected Haymarket mostly but St Margarets had most of the local work to deal with.

When winter came there was a shift back in the links but this change coincided with the annual rail haulage of seed potatoes from Scotland to East Anglia. Sugar beet traffic also brought work to St Margarets along with an increase in demand for coal.

Class K3 and V2 engines undertook the seed potato work but these 'common users' were hard up and sadly neglected as they worked for every depot except their home depot, "64A" on the smokebox door.

Seed potatoes had to be protected from frost so these perishables were transported in vans and insulated with straw. It was quite a sight to see a Class V2 hammering along on the East Coast line with steam blowing at every joint and straw fluttering in the breeze.

With the advent of diesel-electric traction Kings Cross was able to release some of their well kept Green Arrows and these were sent to St Margarets during the '50s. To me as a driver these engines served to prove my workplace and its engines had for long been in a sad state of decay. That's probably why no high ranking official ever came near the place, it had been written off as a lost cause.

In the days of the British Transport Commission when Sir Brian Robertson was at the helm, this former soldier visited St Margarets and created quite a stir. When he came with his entourage to the driver's bothy he stood in the dim light looking at the vast whitewashed walls and disappearing ceiling and said to his escort, "What is this place"? "This is the drivers mess room," replied his escort. "It is a mess, too," said Sir Brian, "we'll have to do something about this!"

Next morning the painters moved in and slapped on chocolate and cream paint, standard colours for railway stations and depots in those days. This paint was quickly absorbed by over a hundred years of whitewash, like ink on blotting paper. After umpteen coats of paint there seemed to be a freshness about the place, a smell of paint instead of body odour and soiled sweat rags. The floor was covered in irregular blobs of a hard mixture of oil and dirt and this mess was scraped off giving a more even surface to a black stone floor. Just as well the table tops were covered with galvanised iron and easily wiped clean, the wooden benches being polished by constant sedentary use.

To succeed as a steam engine driver one had to develop railway sense or, more precisely, locomotive sense. The first signs of this necessary propensity became apparent as a fireman. A young man would concentrate on good firemanship at the expense of other important work and had to be guided by the driver.

I well remember as a passed cleaner I was sent with a driver to turn a Class K3 engine at the Niddrie triangle when St Margarets turntable was out of order. It was a dark night and I felt awkward in a bouncing cab flooded with firelight, my eyes darting from steam pressure gauge to boiler water gauges and back again to steam gauges. The violent twitching of the steam pressure needle and bubbling of water in the gauge glasses made me wonder if all was well. And what about the fire? — shouldn't I be shovelling coal instead of bouncing on the K3's piano stool seat? I looked to my mate for guidance but at the same time hoped I was doing all right.

We went first to Niddrie South then to Niddrie West in the process of turning but we were at Niddrie North and stopped, before a loud voice from the signalbox told me to "Turn that b...... lamp!" In concentrating on firing work I had forgotten the headlamps. The colour of these lamps (red and clear) should have been changed with every change of direction. After that whenever I met that driver he would say, "How's your lamps, Charlie?" As time goes by and more experience is gained these subsidiary jobs became second nature.

Likewise the driver, who would have learned routes and signed the route card accordingly. Sometimes a driver would sign for a stretch of main line signals between two points. If, however, there was a change in routine this driver might be lost if asked to reverse into a siding or do a shunt he was not familiar with. A long firing apprenticeship ensured a driver was well versed in route knowledge.

Chapter 13

Whistle While You Work

The Whistle code was very important in facilitating the movement of trains. There was a large size code book available covering whole areas or a small "Compact Routing Whistle Book" could be carried in a jacket pocket for particular routes.

If for instance I was leaving Edinburgh Waverley station with a train for the Berwick line. I would whistle 1 long 1 short. If heading for the Carlisle line at Portobello East I would whistle 1 long 2 short. Going to Craigentinny Carriage Sidings required 6 short.

A young driver had to know all this but on concentrating on signal sighting he could easily forget to route himself. So you might get the following scenario after a train has been stopped at a signal.

Driver: "Whats the hold up?"

Signalman: "Where are you going?"

Driver: "Fine you b..... ken where I'm going."

Signalman: "What do you think I am, a mind reader? You should use your whistle — route yourself."

Driver: "If I come up there I'll ram a b...... whistle doon your throat!"

Signalman: "Now, now, don't get aggressive, maybe you've not got enough steam to sound your whistle."

With that a poppet safety valve on the boiler top releases excessive pressure and interrupts the conversation making the signalman hurry to pull off the signal and get rid of the deafening noise. Turning to his fireman the driver smiles and says, "That's got rid of him" and the fireman says "Mind when we get to Grantshouse whistle a long and 3 short for water at Berwick''.

'Whistling' is a subsidiary to the actual work in driving a train but just as headlamps become second nature to the fireman whistling becomes a trend of thought not requiring exact concentration. A motorist would call it road sense. Such traits can only be acquired by experience and after many years on the job this experience represents a lot of skill.

Whistling was important to steam railways as a means of communication between driver and signalman long before noise abatement law was thought of. People asleep in their homes at night were a consideration but at certain places like Portobello East and Craigentinny engine whistles were freely used day and night.

As a junction Portobello East had quite a few main line whistles but there were also variations for shunting in the huge marshalling yard. Access to what was known as ''the Centre Road'' called for 6 short whistles and every train being assisted to Waverley or over the Lothian Lines to the Suburban line brought ''cock crows'' from both engines. Craigentinny yard also sounded like a home for roosters as empty coaches left for Waverley Station. In my childhood I lived beside the railway at Dalmeny where every goods train stopped for examination before crossing the Forth Bridge and the continuous clatter of buffers and whistle noise was like a lullaby to me. People troubled with insomnia would no doubt think differently.

There were places where whistling was mandatory and whistle boards were in place to remind drivers but reminders were not needed on the approaches to St Margarets loco depot. In this instance the whistle wasn't so much a warning, more a salute.

Engine whistles popped at regular intervals in St Margarets shed usually preceded by the loud call ''all clear of engine 60951'' (or whatever) as a driver walked around looking for anyone who may be working on the engine. Sometimes a driver would see it as a chance to draw attention to his ego and superior education by substituting the word ''locomotive'' for the more common word "engine". These pop whistles and calls were an important warning but a particular shrill unmusical sound in St Margarets could be unnerving. This happened when an engine was low in steam with the whistle valve open.

The sound, though low, could be heard at a great distance and was very annoying. Anyone in proximity would shut the whistle but very often the wailing sound came from an engine far removed from the centre of operation. In daylight it was possible to look along a row of dead engines and identify the offender by the wisp of steam above the boiler. At night one could only follow the irritating noise and breathe a sigh of relief when the whistle valve was closed and peace restored.

Engines with the whistle handle hanging high were the most common transgressors. The weight of the handle and constant vibrations nearby could cause it to drop allowing low pressure steam to permeate the system. If the handle wouldn't stay closed it was necessary to jam it in that position with a piece of coal. Consequently when the engine was fully active and a driver overcame resistance with a sharp tug at the whistle handle a piece of coal would fall to the cab floor and maybe hit him in the process.

Chapter 14

Practical Yanks

American engine whistles are part of American folklore and have a distinctive drone to match the lethargic style of Americans. This bass sound seems to convey masculine qualities denoting power and strength. After admiring a Gresley A3 at the head of a train it was somewhat disappointing to hear a kind of feminine squeal from the whistle as the train moved off. Not so with his Class A4 or the Stanier engines which had whistle sounds to reflect the power houses they were.

I wouldn't deny Sir Nigel Gresley earned his fame as a railway engineer but there were times when some of his designing brought forth cursing from maintenance men. Some of Gresley's big engines were notorious for wet sand because the sand boxes were located at footplate level where rain water running off the boiler seeped into the sand. On the Gresley three cylinder 2-6-2 tanks of V1 and V3 classes the trailing sand boxes were in the cab, against the back plate, away from dampness. The sand pipe went down through the cab floor to the rear of the trailing driving wheel and was secured by studs on the bottom of the sand box. To gain access to this hidden pipe the floor boards had to be lifted but the pipe was in two parts with a joint in the middle. In order to renew or repair this pipe the joint had to be split and to do this the cab steps had to be removed along with the equalising pipe that ran behind the steps from the front tank to the rear. A major engineering job to remove two ½" bolts that held the halves of the pipes together. This could hardly be classed as a 'running repair'. It required the engine to be stopped and taken out of traffic and in those circumstances a smart foreman would consult the wash-out book and possibly have the boiler washed out while other repairs were effected.

A Gresley engine had a nice appearance but American locos with pipes everywhere were more practical from an enginemans point of view. The Yankee Baldwins I drove in Italy during World War 2 had only one thing in common with Stanier Class 8F's and that was they were both oil burners, though that was a contrast, really.

Whereas the Baldwins were designed as oil burners the British engines were converted coal burners. What took my fancy was the consideration shown to enginemen who had to work these locomotives.

The driving seat was big like an armchair and whistle rope and steam regulator came right into the drivers lap. The fireman didn't have to leave his seat to operate fire controls and injectors. He simply turned on the water handle at floor level and pulled back a short lever, like a car handbrake which controlled the steam. Apart from a water gauge glass on the boiler face there were three taps at different levels which, when opened, allowed boiler water to run into a diagonal trough thus showing true level of water. A gauge glass could give a false reading when grit or some other foreign matter clogged the gauge column cocks but with the tap system the fireman was seeing boiler water under pressure.

There was also a blow-down cock on American engines. At a suitable time and place in open country the fireman would pull a lever and boiler water under pressure would be blasted from the side of the boiler taking away scale and other impurities in the process.

Valve handles on Yankee locomotives were lightweight and air vented which prevented overheating, these could be operated without the risk of burnt fingers bringing forth blisters and loud cursing.

There were some adverse comments regarding the life-span of these very practical American engines but just as their Liberty Boats served their purpose with one crossing of the Atlantic, the Yankee attitude to railways could be summed up in the following semi-official statement:- "The relative life of railroad equipment is generally governed by two factors, operation and maintenance. These factors are usually adverse in military operation and consequently, it is unnecessary to provide refinements to extend the life of this employment over a four or five year period".

The mass production systems in America also influence the life expectancy of their products and whereas the British would say "repair it", the Americans say "replace it". This is sound economics when the amount of capital investment in mass production is considered. It is also more convenient for the military to 'replace' rather than repair.

Chapter 15

Coal Trains

American engines and their like throughout Europe were referred to as Austerities but British locomotive design had been austere since its inception. It wasn't until Gresley provided some cab comfort, such as upholstered seats that the traditional rigorous appearance of steam engines changed. But the Victorian harshness persisted to the very end.

Seats were looked upon as a luxury and when fitted were no more than a piece of wood hinged to the cab side. Many cabs were wide open to the elements but even the closed cabs on former NBR locomotives offered little comfort when moving tender first. This was normal on coal train work when trains weighing about 400 tons were brought from the coal pits at high altitude in the Lothians to docks at sea level at Leith and Granton. Brakes were primitive as in the beginning and were hand operated on wagons and on the engine tender, the engine steam brake being kept in reserve. It was left to the driver to decide how many wagon brakes were needed. These brakes were applied by the guard on wagons next to the engine and it was important to have the train on the move while pinning down brakes. To do otherwise could result in wheels sliding instead of turning causing flats on tyres.

Apply Wagon Brakes (AWB) instructions were contained in the operating orders and there were wooden markers at the appropriate points. When the time came to lift the wagon brakes the guard would hurry forward with his brake stick (not shunting pole) and do the necessary, sometimes the fireman would do the job for the guard.

On the steep descent from the colliery the driver would feel the weight of the train cushioning up and apply the tender handbrake accordingly. The guard in his van at the end of the train would be "toying" with his handbrake, checking the brake power at his disposal. He had to be careful to avoid strain on the train couplings and guard against breaking a coupling by a sudden tug; likewise the driver had to drive with great care ever mindful of guards' presence and vulnerability in his trailing van. Many guards sustained injury while working slack coupled trains.

There was a time during the 50s when vacuum fitted coal wagons were introduced. But these automatic brakes were found to be unsuitable in collieries not designed for such vehicles. These big red wagons, newly built, were stored in a siding that was once a single line linking Smeaton Jct and Hardengreen Jct, before eventually going to the scrap yard.

Coal train working on a sunny spring morning was an opportunity to discover Nature's blessings, wild animals close to the track and domesticated beasts beyond the fences that kept them away from the railway. I remember entering Portobello loop with a coal train and my fireman screwing down the tender handbrake on a Class J37. George was a man of few words and had only spoken two words; "Good morning" since starting work. So it came as a surprise when he commented on a rabbit crossing the railway embankment. "That must be a thrifty rabbit, Charlie" said George. Feeling startled at hearing his voice I managed to ask "Why do you say that, George?" and turning to face me in the cab, he said, "Because it keeps it's doe in the railway bank".

Things were somewhat different on a dark and stormy night cowering behind a storm sheet with backs against the boiler. The storm sheet, a flimsy piece of tarpaulin, was usually rolled and tied to the cab roof. The weather had to be really bad before men would unroll this sheet, stretch it out and secure it to fixtures on the tender. It was effective to some extent but a strong wind would drive rain and snow in from the sides and signals were difficult to sight.

On the 1 in 70 descent from Lady Victoria Pit with a coal train there was a need for good and intelligent braking. Usually we had a Class J37 running tender first. The all important tender handbrake was set low enough to exert full arm and body pressure, one felt one was really on top of the job with a Class J37. The Gresley Class J38 had a high tender and consequently the handbrake was high and did not lend itself to the same pressure, although this engine and tender were 7 tons heavier than the Class J37. Occasionally the Class J35, some weighing less than 76 tons were on coal train work and it was on one of these "lightweights" I ran away one day, it was running "smokebox leading" instead of the usual "tender leading".

Chapter 16

The Runaway

I realised this train was out of control soon after the full weight buffered up to the engine on the 1 in 70 falling gradient, even the "reserve" steam brake failed to impede the hair raising descent and a series of pop whistles to the guard brought no assistance from the back. As the runaway train bucked and heaved I prayed the Hardengreen Junction Down Distant signal would be set in my favour. This signal was positioned round a bend and my relief was immense when I saw the fish-tail arm pointing to the sky. Hardengreen was a very busy junction serving the Peebles branch line as well as the Waverley Route and had something stood in my way it would have been a disaster.

It was a disaster for a colleague of mine, Jim Harkins, on the 10 November 1955 on a gradient of 1 in 55 on the Glencorse Branch. He was working a heavy coal train with Class J38 0-6-0 No 65906 on the single line from Loanhead to Millerhill, one of the most difficult railways in the Edinburgh area.

The tricky part was the levelling out at Gilmerton, about halfway. In accordance with the rules, a number of wagon brakes were to be pinned down on the front of the train at the summit, near to Straiton Sidings, to enable the train to be brought to a stand at the bridge crossing the Edinburgh-Lasswade road, where more wagon brakes were to be pinned down, prior to the final descent.

As the 'J38' approached Straiton Sidings, working its 35 wagon load tender leading, the men on the footplate heard a strange noise that prompted Fireman J H Scott to climb out on to the running plate to inspect. He discovered that the brake-blocks were hanging away from the driving wheels, and on the 1 in 67 gradient the train was starting to run away.

In fearful abandon nearly 400 tons of coal pushed the loco relentlessly from behind and without means of controlling the fierce impetus Driver Harkins can be excused for failing to keep a cool head.

The prospect of ending up under the engine and a mountain of coal and wagons, prompted the driver to "abandon ship". As the J38 rushed on trailing those bucking coal wagons at about 40 m.p.h. Harkins jumped on to the rising embankment and hit the ground with fierce impact. There was no chance of holding on to the stilted turf and his shock-racked body slithered down the grassy slope and under the wheels of the raging coal wagons where death was instantaneous.

Fireman Scott jumped, too, and sustained only cuts and bruises but the guard stayed with the train. We can well wonder what his thoughts were as the runaway raced into the unknown.

Signalman Bell at Millerhill, looking at his panel, saw the light come on as the coal train operated the track circuit. He knew that to divert the train into the station dock would cause a frightful crash so he decided to throw the lever allowing the runaway onto the main line. As it passed the signalbox the train was beginning to steady and on the rising gradient to Niddrie South it finally came to rest. The guard survived, but 12 children were left fatherless as a result of the drivers death.

A later inquiry found that a brake pull-rod between trailing and leading driving wheels had broken, making the entire engine brake useless. The fault was caused by the brake rod being beaten by the movement of an engine crank through insufficient clearance, a weakness in design.

The Class J38 0-6-0, a Gresley design to deal with coal traffic in Scotland was introduced in 1926, a total of 35 locomotives. A redesigned brake gear was fitted to these engines and began in 1953. At the time of the accident 31 of the 35 locos had been dealt with, No 65906 was one of the four engines that hadn't been altered.

The most precarious railway worked by St Margarets men must surely have been the Gas Works single line at Granton. This railway was built into the side of a grassy embankment a steep slope of mounds and ridges hiding the tortuous gradient from sea level.

There was a semaphore signal near the foot of the Branch to regulate trains and engines passing from the Harbour Line to the Gas Works and a gong was fixed near the Pointsman's box at Royston Level Crossing — about 100 yards — outside the Gas Works gate, to be worked by a lever placed near the signal-post.

All trains and engines proceeding in the direction of the Gas Works had to be brought to a stand at the foot of the Branch and the shunter, guard, or fireman would give two beats on the gong to let the Pointsman know that a train was ready to proceed up the Branch; the Pointsman would then pull off the signal if the line was clear. Should the Pointsman not respond the beats on the gong had to be repeated at short intervals.

Before opening the signal the Pointsman had to satisfy himself that the line was clear to the Gas Works Siding and also that the Level Crossing was not occupied. When propelling wagons up the Branch the trainmen had to keep a sharp lookout and be prepared to stop at any obstruction.

The wee pug would collect five loaded wagons from coal trains stabled in the Harbour sidings and position these at the foot of the Branch. By this time there was a good head of steam and near full boiler. When the signal was lowered the J88 would charge like a bull on to the incline and seemed to roar like a bull as soon as the load pressed hard against the buffers. The initial run-in built up speed to overcome the steep curvature of the line and soon the whistle blasted a warning to Royston Level Crossing. Once passed that handicap it was an easier run into the Gas Works Sidings.

The descent from this place would also be hazardous

with the 38 ton J88 trying to hold back 20 or more heaving wagons loaded with breeze, a by-product from coal gas production. This is when wagon brakes were all important and it was comforting to see a shunter with strong hands pinning down the brake handles as the train moved forward to the brow of the hill.

One day as this preparation work was in progress a worker asked me for a lift down to the "Square", meaning Granton Square the tram car terminus adjacent to the railway goods yard. As I nodded approval he jumped into the engine cab and stood with his back against the coal bunker dreamily watching the flickering flames in the wee firebox.

As the shunter pinned down the wagon brakes my fireman put on the engine handbrake and I afforded further control with the steam brake. Soon we were on the hill and being pushed mercilessly by the heavy train. There was no guards brake van, the shunters rode "side-saddle" on a brake stick jammed into a wagon. It was like a bucking bronco on that pug and I could see wagons doing a shuttle movement on every bend and threatening to mount the engine. I recalled a similar runaway the previous week when the loco failed to take the bend at the bottom and ended smashed up with the wagons on the beach.

There was no chance of stopping at the prescribed spot at the foot of the hill and when I saw the shunters jumping wildly from their perches on to grassy slopes I knew there was no-one to stop road traffic and escort the train across the road. All I could do was bang away at the whistle, a mushroom shaped attachment, and hope for the best.

All this time the passenger stood dreamily gazing into the fire and even at the bottom when we hit the curve and took a severe jolt the dreamer merely grabbed the hand brake handle and steadied himself. As we slowed on the Harbour Line I finally got the train under control and wondered at my quiet surroundings, there was no motor or horse traffic, only an occasional pedestrian. Soon, we stopped and all was still and I realised it was a public holiday which was why the usual activity was missing. Nonchalantly, our passenger climbed down from the cab saying, "Thanks driver, some people are lucky being on holiday." Lucky! — he didn't realise how good fortune had smiled on us on that runaway train.

Chapter 17

Crashes and Cranes

The history of railways must include a record of accidents
and disasters. It was imperative that a means was afforded
to deal with such happenings. Consequently, breakdown
cranes and tool vans were located at strategic points to
attend mishaps over a wide area. St Margarets had a heavy
lifting crane built by Cowans, Sheldon in 1914 with a
capacity of 36 tons. This crane had six axles and was
constantly in steam ready for action, the crew on hand,
fitters and fitters mates, labourers and shed workers.
When called out during the night men at home were
alerted by a young messenger and were usually on the job
before the messenger returned to shed. The crane driver
was always in attendance and ready for action. When
called out the breakdown crane or tool van had priority
over other jobs both for engines and exiting from shed. A
senior foreman was always in attendance and the shedmas-
ter went out with the crane.

When first built in 1914 the crane number was 971,567
and to the order of the NBR Company. This crane first
went to Thornton in 1914 and to Kittybrewster in 1927
while St Margarets had a smaller crane built by Cowans in
1897 with a capacity of 15 tons with 4 axles which was
withdrawn in 1949.

In 1961 an ex LMS crane, built by Cowans in 1930,
came to St Margarets from Motherwell and in 1966
went to Haymarket. There were inter-depot changes with
cranes just as with steam locomotives. A crane gave a
depot improved status so that in steam days from
1949 St Margarets was 64A and Haymarket 64B. Likewise

Thornton was 62A, Dundee 62B.

At its peak St Margarets was, in effect, a North British Railway Co live museum. This was where it all started in 1846, locos, carriages, wagons were all part of the scene throughout this depots' long history in the east end of Edinburgh. The NBR depot in the west end of Scotlands' capital city was a later development, about half a century later. Haymarket took its name from that particular district in Edinburgh along with a goods yard and passenger station, practically in alignment towards the east.

Chapter 18

Haymarket Motive Power Depot

I find on looking back in life I can associate particular places with peculiar smells. St Margarets in a hollow brings to mind a concoction of soot and hot oil whereas Haymarket on a higher level was affected by the fragrant mixture emanating from surrounding industries — beer, whisky, and confectionery.

As a telephone attendant at that depot in 1935 I sat at a tall sloping desk close to where supervisors taking duty read the log book. There was no aftershave in those days but I was able to sense the scrubbed freshness of personal hygiene and the smell of a gaffer's raincoat.

In contrast to St Margaret's antiquity, Haymarket at that time was experiencing a new awakening with the arrival of Gresley Pacifics. The Class A3 had for long been resident at Haymarket and I remember as a boy at Dalmeny in 1929 the mystique of Gresleys experimental "Hush-Hush" No 10,000 was on everybodys lips. This monster soon disappeared from the scene and was rebuilt in conventional style in 1938.

Meantime the P2's were arriving, No 2001 Cock o'the North leading the way with its 2-8-2 wheel arrangement to challenge the tortuous Aberdeen Road. Then flowed Lord President, Mons Meg, Thane of Fife, Wolf of Badenoch and Earl Marischal. These engines created keen interest and when I saw the firebox of No 2001 I thought "there's room in there to have a dance", Tommy McGowan was one of the first Haymarket firemen to take on the challenge of feeding coal to the hungry "Cock" and being of small stature Tommy required a wooden stool to reach

81

the water injector steam handle. The big combustion chamber combined with a 2-8-2 arrangement harnessing smaller driving wheels designed to haul heavy passenger trains at speed over tortuous terrain was not a success and these locos were rebuilt by Edward Thompson who became the LNER Chief Mechanical Engineer after Gresley's death in 1941. But Gresley's A4's and V2's quickly made up for any miscalculations on Sir Nigel's part.

Soon Haymarket engine crews were journeying to Doncaster to collect their allocation and Norman McKillop (alias Toram Beg) was rightly proud of his participation in this work. Being technically minded and well versed in the history of steam locomotives Norman's interest in the A4's was more than a passing fancy. He had a wide experience of NE and NBR engines and knew when something of significance was happening in the railway world. Gresley products were magnificently significant. Although a thoroughbred Englishman, Sir Nigel was in fact born in Edinburgh on 19th June 1876 within half a mile of Waverley station where his engines dominated the scene for nearly half a century.

Gresley Pacifics had rolled steel tyres which were sometimes subject to fracture on the 6ft 8ins diameter driving wheels. But it was not just a crack that one Haymarket driver experienced, the whole tyre came off the left driving wheel while speeding down Cockburns path and he was on the turntable at Haymarket when he noticed this particular driving wheel had something missing.

The engine was not running on spokes but on the rim of the wheel proper, which in itself was a complete casting onto which the tyre was sweated. This was in contrast to the American austerity locos built in large numbers during World War 2, their wheels and tyres were in a single cast and when they became flat due to wheel lock on braking the crew in the cab knew all about it.

On another occasion an engine came on shed with part of a wooden sleeper lodged in the water scoop.

Water pick up gear in St Margarets was of little consequence to enginemen or maintenance staff unless of course an examiner spotted a major defect. At Haymarket, however, such fittings were regularly tested and oiled, the scoop properly secured in the up position ready for use at Lucker Troughs South of Berwick.

I find pleasure in remembering my short sojourn at Haymarket, first as a toolstore boy and later a telephone attendant. In between these occupations I was redundant and employed outwith the railway service.

History has logged this period as the "hungry 30's", there was a great depression which spawned tremendous unemployment and wholesale redundancies. Young people starting their working lives were superfluous to requirements soon after being employed. As an alternative to the scrap heap cleaners were offered and accepted work on the permanent way. Consequently, cleaners at Haymarket and elsewhere who should have been on firing work and in the line of promotion were somewhat elderly, possibly verging on 30.

Despite this economic crisis those years brought glory and distinction to Haymarket in the form of super locomotives manned by dedicated enginemen.

I truly wish that today's steam enthusiast could feel as privileged as I felt on my first day at Haymarket, an 8.00 am start, lined up outside the shed at this time there could be eight magnificent Pacifics in a state of preparation. Their names were legion, successors of Derby winners over the years — Windsor Lad, Hyperion, Cameronian, Salmon Trout, Brown Jack, Knight of Thistle, Grand Parade — a grand parade indeed.

The race horse and the Gresley Pacific made a harmonious union not only in name but in style. Each were full of vibrant life and were fed, watered and "trained".

There was much human activity too, in preparing these engines for long distance hauls at high speed. They gobbled up the best quality coal and demanded a superior lubrication. While firing shovels clattered in every cab as the fires were built up smoke rocketed to the sky. Drivers armed with oil pouries diligently poured lubricant into the motions and axle boxes. Cleaners added sheen to an already shining locomotive. Fitters did last minute repairs and midst all this cacophony could be heard the regular sound of the examiners' hammer tapping wheels and other parts. Then when all was ready firemen would fix headboards at chimney level. Flying Scotsman, The Fair Maid, Capitals Limited, The Elizabethan. Haymarket was indeed 'elite', engines and enginemen were the best.

Chapter 19

Morning Races

The main line through St Margarets had a permanent speed restriction for obvious reasons, not so the main line adjacent to Haymarket steam depot. Trains from the North and West ran at high speed towards Waverley station. There was a footpath alongside the Up line giving access to Haymarket station. It lay at a lower level than the well ballasted main line and allowed a close view of the spinning wheels on passing locos, just like watching a model railway.

Under what was known as the Caley Bridge the track was on a bend and it was a fascinating sight to watch an approaching train negotiate this slight curve, the engine moved sideways like a shuttle, straightened up then charged on.

In the early morning there was usually an audience at Haymarket shed to see the race between the 7.30 am Glasgow and 7.30 am Aberdeen. These two trains left Edinburgh abreast of each other and after passing through tunnels emerged into the light at Haymarket station still neck and neck. Enginemen and guards all participated in the race so it was as a team the two trains departed from Haymarket station both with Pacific engines. By the time they reached the shed the staccato beat of the two engines had blended in six soft beats from each and acceleration had quickened. At Saughton Junction the Glasgow train veered to the left while the Aberdeen train followed the route to the North. All this time the firemen had been urging the engines on like racehorse jockeys using a whip, the persuaders being the water spray pipes used for damping coal and dust. As the trains parted company at Saughton Junction the enginemen exchanged waves and whistled and a keen observer might see the firemen pick up their shovels and bend their backs while the drivers tugged on the steam regulator to make sure it was fully open. Although the contest was over the race against time had just begun.

Haymarket shed with eight roads and open ends was more spacious than St Margarets but restricted, nevertheless. The big advantage at Haymarket was the mechanical coaling plant. This concrete monster was in good condition when I first made its acquaintance. Coal was dispensed at the touch of a button and tonnage recorded on small scrolls. Every morning the coal clerk removed these rolls of paper and transferred the information to his book in the general office. There were two hoppers, one of which could be used to hold special coal for the "non-stop" i.e, the Flying Scotsman — The Capitals Ltd — and The Elizabethan according to a particular period.

Charlie Reid was the Mechanical Plant Attendant responsible for keeping hoppers full in my time. Coal was stored in wagons on raised ground which allowed the wagons to move by gravity and be positioned by Reid on the lifting platform. Then at the press of a button the whole wagon would be raised to the top of the plant and tipped into a hopper.

Some coaling plants were differently designed. Thornton, for instance had the wagon tipped into a large bucket then the bucket was raised at a high level to be tipped into a hopper.

During frosty weather the machinery was kept in order by heat from braziers suitably positioned.

Night work with steam locomotives threw new light on the job — firelight! My first ride on the footplate at night was on the A3 Pacific No 60078 (BR number) appropriately named Night Hawk. This was a Gateshead engine booked to work the 11.30 pm parcels train from Waverley station, a train popularly known as the "dog and monkey" because of the miscellaneous goods carried.

I had just finished back shift at 10.00 pm and was heading for home in the east end of Edinburgh when Night Hawk moved towards the outlet signal. I knew the driver and fireman and stood behind the driver holding on to his bucket seat. After phoning the signalman the fireman quickly returned to his place in the cab and the ground signal turned to green and there were other green signals beyond tracing over route to Waverley station.

As the fierce white-hot fire set its searchlight beam to the sky Night Hawk rattled over points and crossings before setting a course on the South Up main line where the running was smooth and noise minimal. Passing through Haymarket station the mechanical sounds reverberated between platforms and echoed louder as Night Hawk entered the tunnel.

Here the fire-glare was trapped and spread out across the tunnel roof revealing the soot covered stonework. As we passed under the air ventilators built inside the tunnel the fireglow disappeared for fleeting seconds up the ventilator shaft.

Passing through Princes Street Gardens the echoing mechanical sound took on a new note as it travelled further to the castle rock before rebounding into the gardens. Then came the enclosed echo again as we passed through the Mound tunnel into the brilliantly lit Waverley station. We were routed via the suburban line, which lay in darkness, towards the east end of the station and again the "Gresley Knock" echoed in the close confines of the platform and roof when Night Hawk stopped opposite the exit steps. I alighted just as the poppet safety valves released 220 lbs pressure which was cut off when the fireman opened the water injector. Looking back from the staircase I could see the name Night Hawk deep in shadows, an appropriate surround.

I used to enjoy Sunday work when I was on the telephones at Haymarket. Things were quieter on Sunday but it was then many strange Pacifics came in from distant parts down south. This is when I joined the disposal enginemen under their guidance and had the opportunity to drive. After turning a loco the disposal driver would sit on the fireman's seat and allow me to drive these Pacifics as far as the coaling plant where inconspicuous markings indicated stopping point. The highlight of these memorable days was when No 4472 Flying Scotsmen came in from Kings Cross and I drove it that short distance.

Chapter 20

'One Up His Sleeve'

Train engines could fail on shed or away from shed for a variety of reasons and cause great disruption. A conscientious foreman would allow for such an emergency and have a spare engine 'up his sleeve' as they used to say. There were spare engine crews on duty throughout the 24 hours but it was not always possible to match them with an engine. At St Margarets there was the added requirement of catering for the breakdown crane although this work had priority over everything and usually acquired the first suitable engine.

It was not unusual to see a Class Y9 saddle tank pug dashing to a breakdown with a toolvan but a heavy crane called for a heavy engine. When the Control alerted the loco depot to an emergency a lethargic gaffer might say, "I've nothing here, the place is empty" and go back to sleep. A more worthy foreman would plan ahead for such a crisis and be ready for an urgent call.

I found when acting foreman at St Margarets extra effort could pay dividends. there was rarely a spare engine in steam but the shed was full of dead engines in for repairs or boiler washing. It was a daunting task to shunt St Margarets shed because of the proximity of the busy main line and shunts got low priority.

The thing to do was to "take the bull by the horns", assemble as many enginemen as possible and dig out a dead engine ready for traffic. On seeing what was happening the signalman would turn pale and had to be assured there would be no hitches.

I was in the signalbox one Sunday when a shunt on to

the main line was requested. This coincided with news that an express train from Kings Cross was at Dunbar, 30 miles away. When the loco shunt was requested the signalman said "Aye, hawd on I've got the fast coming". This is what St Margarets gaffers were up against all the time causing them to renege on shed shunting. If enginemen were allocated to big shunts there were less men available to deal with engines arriving in the coal store. So it was some kind of achievement to uncover an engine in the shed that had been waiting a long time to be resuscitated. Furthermore, I felt elated as I went about my duties with an eye on a very useful engine coming into steam. I was also creating work for spare men lounging in bothies who appeared affronted when instructed to prepare an engine that had been immobilised for weeks.

Such an engine would require much cleaning and would consume gallons of oil. Fitters would have to be called to replace parts missing through cannibalism and the whole effort would be in vain if, after all this a major defect was discovered. Little wonder my chest swelled with satisfaction when I saw such an engine move towards the outlet signal on its way to work after a very long rest.

Chapter 21

Thornton Aye Ready

Thornton steam shed had two Class B1's prepared in case of emergency which included the breakdown crane. Because of its geographical position half way between Edinburgh and Dundee and passenger train activity at Thornton station it was not unusual to receive a call for assistance. These B1's were also useful to transport fitters to the scene of a breakdown.

As a driver I was working a freight train from Niddrie to Dundee with a Stanier Class 5. Like their sisters the 8F's, which I handled while serving in Italy during WW2, they were good engines but had a serious fault — water injectors. We had trouble with the right injector soon after leaving St Margarets and at Forth Bridge North I advised the Control we would require a fresh engine at Thornton. Sure enough we were diverted into the Down Loop at Thornton Station signalbox where we changed over with a Thornton Class B1 and continued our journey to Dundee.

The B1's in reserve at Thornton steam shed had to be kept at the ready if they were to serve their purpose. They had to be coaled and watered, fires cleaned and motions oiled at regular intervals but they were handy for shunting on the shed as well as helping out on the main line.

Gresley's successor, Edward Thompson, was responsible for the design on the Class B1 a simple two-cylinder mixed traffic 4-6-0 locomotive built to a total of over 400 between 1941 and 1949. It compared favourably with the Stainer Class 5 especially in creature comforts. Thompson had moved away from Gresley's conjugated gear preferring a more simple design and dispensing with complicated diagnosis of faults and awkward repairs.

There was no mistaking a Gresley three cylinder "off the beat" as it was called when six equal exhaust beats became irregular pulsations due to change in valve setting. This was an opportunity for a mechanically minded driver to determine the actual fault by testing steam flow at particular wheel settings.

The Walschaert Valve Gear controlled the steam events in the two cylinders but with Gresley's conjugated three cylinders locomotive where gear for the outside cylinders operate the inside cylinders through a system of levers things were more complicated. After the defect had been diagnosed and repairs effected the valve setting had to be tested. This called for highly skilled judgement by a foreman fitter who would stand and listen as the driver moved the locomotive and operated the reverser at various settings to change the cut-off through the expansion link, a long vertical slot, a kind of curved steel frame which housed the die block actuated by the radius rod attached to the valve spindle crosshead moved by piston valve heads in the small cylinder above the main piston cylinder. This link up of levers reminded me of the song "the knee bone's connected to the leg bone...." but it was all part of learning the steam locomotive.

Every major steam locomotive depot had a Mutual Improvement Class (MIC) which depended entirely on self motivation. Management at one time showed little interest in training workers, it was left to the men themselves to teach and learn. Long after nationalisation of railways BR organised competitions between MIC teams and created further interest. But mainly it was left to keen locomotivemen to organise classes and encourage others.

St Margarets first MIC accommodation was an old NBR carriage body located close to the main line at Piershill Junction and within sight of signalbox and engine depot. There was longitudinal communal seating alongside the wall and windows while passing trains and black smoke created atmosphere for the subject being taught. Meetings were in the evening or Sunday afternoon.

Andrew Anderson, a young driver, was secretary who did all the organising and kept the classroom clean.

The teaching sessions were relaxed and in this mood potential enginemen more easily absorbed what had to be learnt, that is the steam locomotive, rules and regulations. Instruction became more intense for an individual when he was due to undergo a test for firing or driving before the examining inspector. If a man required extra tuition there was always a volunteer to coach him at home.

Promotion was fast at St Margarets during the war when I was a "D Day Dodger" out in Italy driving Stanier 8F's and Yankee Baldwin oil burning locomotives. It was a condition of my release from the LNER into the Royal Engineers as a volunteer for military service that I returned to St Margarets on being demobilised. So, in 1946 I was restored to my place in the links, although I still had to pass my driving test.

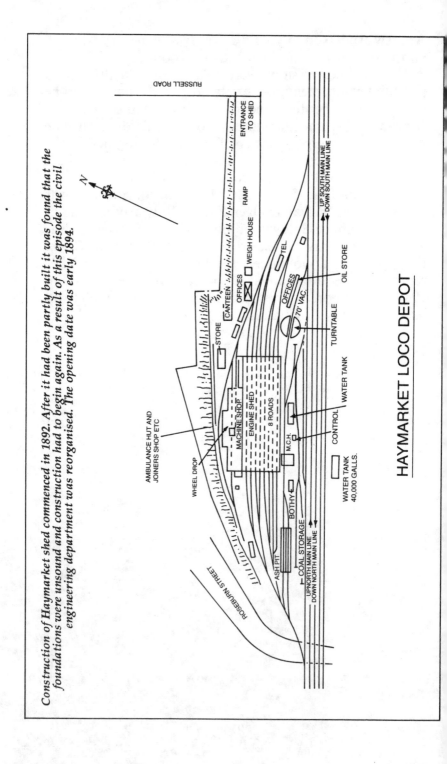

Construction of Haymarket shed commenced in 1892. After it had been partly built it was found that the foundations were unsound and construction had to begin again. As a result of this episode the civil engineering department was reorganised. The opening date was early 1894.

HAYMARKET LOCO DEPOT

Chapter 22

The Driving Test

John Bartholomew was the chief locomotive Inspector located at Waverley. A former driver at St Margarets and Haymarket John was a real gentleman. When I entered his office that Friday morning in 1947 feeling somewhat tense he immediately put me at ease with his friendly "Hello, Charlie, take your coat off, come and sit down". We then started a conversation about life in general and soon he was asking definite questions about the steam locomotive — boiler, firebox, brakes and gearing, the lot.

Then we progressed on to the rules and regulations with emphasis on single line working and wrong line orders. The former was a complicated business which could arise from various situations and one question that stuck in my mind was, "You are the driver on the leading engine of a double headed train — who collects the token, your authority to occupy the single line?"

I had experienced plenty of single line working on military railways when regulations had little in common with British railways but this double heading situation demanded some thought. I had to recall an MIC meeting to come up with the right answer which is, "The token is carried on the second engine after the leading driver has seen it and checked that the token applied to the section of single line being used."

It was pay day for John Bartholomew so my agony was not prolonged. Soon I was signing the Board of Trade register as a qualified steam engine driver. John gave me a pile of books relative to rules and regulations and I went on my way with a song in my heart.

The practical test for St Margarets men was conducted out on the suburban passenger trains. So it was I found myself accompanied by a colleague Dick Watson and Inspector James Nixon on a Class V1 side tank engine. The inspector told me to sit in the train while Dick took over the controls from the regular driver Joe McCann. My turn would be between Duddingston and Waverley station.

When we reached the "brewery district" I went forward and relieved Dick Watson, while Joe McCann stood at my back with a critical look in his eyes. I was conscious of intense concentration as I sought to perfect my performance. The inspector sat on the fireman's seat with his head out of the window apparently unconcerned. I diligently viewed the steam gauge and water level in the boiler, checked the vacuum gauge reading and tried to appear relaxed as I awaited a wave from the guard. When this came I acknowledged with a smart toot on the whistle and opened the steam regulator. At this point I recalled Norman McKillops' work study ideas. He maintained time was saved by applying steam first then whistling.

The V1 Class loco had quick acceleration and was ideal for suburban work and umpteen stops and starts. As I adjusted the reverser to an economical 'cut off' (good text book stuff this) Sandy Henderson, the fireman, sidled up to me and whispered "Take it easy Charlie, we don't want to be going into Haymarket for coal". I had to contend with his funny asides all the way to Waverley, I was sore laughing. All this time the inspector looked out of the window.

When we alighted at Waverley and went to the staff canteen the inspector made it clear he hadn't been asleep. His criticism was constructive but in my case impracticable. "You, Charlie", he said, "should have tested your brake after taking over at Duddingston". This was theoretically sound advice but with Joe McCann at my back eyeing his watch and my performance it wasn't a good idea to impede the speed of the train. Joe was a senior driver with a temperament to match his status. Any interference with the running of the train would have had Joe chasing us off the footplate along with the inspector.

Chapter 23

The Gaffer

In 1956 I started doing relief supervisory work, running foreman at St Margarets, locomotive inspector at Waverley station, John Bartholomew had retired from the railway and had a job with Patrick Thomsons, a large departmental store on North Bridge above the Waverley. Every day before going to "PT's" he would sit beside the statue of John Walker former manager of the North British Railway Company (NBR). I always spoke with him in the passing but one day he came into my office and told me a story.

Away back about 1910 when he was a cleaner laddie at St Margarets he was sent to Polton, a sub-depot, to caretake the engine there, the usual caretaker being off work sick. There was no liaison van in those days and John had to walk to Polton, about 14 miles. When he came to Hardengreen Junction he asked for directions and was sent along the Peebles branch towards his destination.

When he reached Polton long after midnight he was exhausted and fell fast asleep in the bothy.

He then became aware of being shakened and rudely awakened. It was the Polton driver in a rage demanding to know why his engine was dead and without fire.

At this point of John's story he moved towards the mirror and adjusted his Paisley pattern silk scarf. "Aye, Charlie", he said, "all Polton had a late start that morning but I've never looked back since".

As locomotive inspector at Waverley I was responsible for the engines and enginemen in that environment. To the men themselves I was the "black smoke inspector" but watching for air pollution was only one of my duties albeit an important one. I had to ensure that locomotives were in order and ready to depart timeously. I also had to meet the more important trains on arrival and check on any late running or unusual occurrence. Liaison with Control was very important and particularly with the 'loco man' in that organisation.

This gent phoned one day and asked me to interview the driver of the Elizabethan non-stop and ask why he stopped at Grantshouse for water. It seemed a silly question but I went ahead and met the so called 'non-stop' on arrival. I was keen to see the drivers reaction to the question.

The driver that day was one of Norman McKillop's "Enginemen Elite" Bill Nairn, a big former Scots Guardsman. "Hello Bill," I said as I entered the cab of No 60031 Golden Plover "are you missing No 4?" (a reference to his own engine No 60004 William Whitelaw). "No", said Bill, "this is a good engine but her bladder's a bit weak, she uses a lot of water". I could see he looked a bit down in the mouth and I hesitated before putting Control's query to him. "The Control wants to know, Bill, why you stopped for water at Grantshouse". All the pent-up indignation he had felt at having to stop the 'non-stop suddenly exploded and he raged: "F... the Control, tell them I stopped for a pee!", and in the same breath said, "tell the signalman I'll be taking water at the end of the platform to see this engine through disposal".

Gone was the glamour associated with express passenger trains. Bill Nairn must have been wishing he was on the Haymarket pilot and carefree.

At 10 o'clock in the morning there was a line up of big engines at Waverley west end — the Aberdeen, Glasgow and Perth all simmering and raring to go. The sight of the black smoke inspector was enough to keep the reek under control but as these trains moved towards the Mound tunnel the firemen would push the heaped fire over the bars causing an alarming mushroom of black smoke. As a result shopkeepers and residents in Princes Street came on the phone complaining and threatening to report the matter to the city's Health Officer.

There were quiet spells on the Waverley job when I found refuge in a small office away from the maddening throng of a busy rail station. I was sitting in this peaceful retreat one afternoon when the door opened and a driver who I recognised as a Newcastle man said, "Maybe this inspector can help" and ushered in a lady whose style belied her maturity.

Chapter 24

An Old Love

She wore a summer straw hat with flowers atop her fair hair. Her dress of pale yellow satin oozed elegance and her quality shoes elevated her well proportioned body.

"Please sit down" I said, offering a chair for this purpose, "how can I help you?" As she gracefully adopted a sedentary position she looked shyly towards me and quietly said, "I'm on a quick visit to Edinburgh and I would like to meet an old acquaintance who I understand is an engine driver, his name is Bob Mackie, I wonder if you know him? My name is Mrs Corsar I live in London."

Mrs Corsar went on to explain that many years ago she and Bob Mackie were engaged to be married but for no apparent reason they drifted apart and their destinies were fashioned elsewhere. She married and settled in England, Bob Mackie married and stayed in Edinburgh.

"Mrs Corsar", I said "this must be your lucky day, your former fiance is sitting on an engine in No 4 platform preparing to work the 4.10 pm Hawick. Come with me and I'll take you to him", and together we left the office.

As we approached the Scott Class engine "Laird o' Monkbarns" at the head of the train I could see the fireman on the ground attaching a hose pipe to a hydrant preparing to water the coal. In the cab Bob was sitting looking mournfully towards St Andrews House high on a rock once occupied by the Calton Jail.

"Bob!", I called "here's someone to see you". As Bob crossed the cab Mrs Corsar stood on tiptoes for a better view. There was instant recognition between the two and just faint blushing. As I retraced my steps passing the fireman on the ground I said "Hello, Willie, don't be in a hurry to rejoin your engine". Willie looked at me in wonderment, but I said no more.

I returned to Platform 4 as the Hawick train disappeared towards the Calton Tunnel and people left the platform. She was just one in the crowd wiping a tear-stained face, I felt privileged to share her secret.

The Waverley station now is strangled with modernity. There is no longer the vibrating vitality of steam days when smart wee shunting engines dressed in apple green made short work of splitting up passenger trains from the south and placing portions for Perth and Aberdeen in their respective berths.

No longer do we see strong shunters carrying heavy vestibule covers from one platform to another; the line up of "pauchling" porters and other grades waiting to carry baggage and earn the price of a drink has long ago disappeared; with this, too, went a sight that heartened every steam enthusiast. Looking beyond the east and of No 10/11 platform, the old Down Main, one could see the wedged nose front of a Class A4 emerging from Calton Tunnel with the "Elizabethan" headboard and just a trace of exhaust at the chimney. After a gentle twist in the line the A4 steadied on a straight course and rolled to a stop near the middle of No 11 platform.

Whenever I saw the wheels turning on that last lap I thought, those wheels have been going round non stop since leaving Kings Cross 400 miles away, that is providing the engine didn't stop for water at Grantshouse or elsewhere.

Lack of water was often a problem with this train. Sometimes the troughs at Lucker, south of Berwick were low, resulting in the engine tank not being properly filled. On one occasion the injectors blew off passing through St Margarets and on reaching Waverley the engine had to be quickly uncoupled to allow it to run forward and take on water. This called for fast action from all concerned.

I was a spare driver at St Margarets one day when news came that the Elizabethan engine had failed at Dunbar with a hot axle box. The Dunbar Class D49 Shire had replaced the A4 which meant assistance at St Margarets for the 1 in 78 climb to Waverley.

I was detailed to take a Class V1 off the end of the coal store and stand by ready to assist. When the Shire limped to a stand at the Down Home signal with the "Elizabethan" headboard at the chimney I took the V1 to the front of the Shire and my mate quickly coupled on. Soon we were going up that hill in style and without effort.

At Waverley there was a large crowd waiting to meet this shamed prestige train but I felt good with all those eyes on me and the humble V1. Dunbar men had travelled on the train to take the Shire back to Dunbar but the Haymarket men insisted on taking the engine to Haymarket thereby maximising their mileage money.

In 1948 when flooding closed the East Coast route trains were diverted via the Waverley Route. This increased mileage meant higher water consumption but rather than stop at a convenient water supply some Haymarket men carried on to Lucker Troughs.

Most of them required conductors and this made work for St Margarets men who were familiar with the Waverley Route and the outlet to Berwick via Kelso.

Chapter 25

Banking Engines

Although Waverley station was primarily for passenger traffic the place was used intensively at night as a throughway for freight trains to north and west. These long heavy trains came from Leith and Portobello and had banking engines to assist them. At the departure point the assisting engine would lead the way then at South Leith Junction this engine was in the rear. When signals showed green and "cock-crow" whistles had been exchanged the train moved off towards Waverley at a moderate speed. Usually a Class J36 was pushing from behind and as the train approached Peirshill Junction the driver looked out for the St Margarets distant semaphore signal on a high gantry. This signal in the off position was an indication to the assisting driver to open wide the steam regulator after 'notching up' the reverser, a lever type which engaged with notches in the quadrant.

The train soon built up speed sufficient to overcome the rising gradient ahead and as we roared through St Margarets with smoke and sparks rocketing to the sky the sound reverberating from high tenements, men waiting to cross the main line or standing nearby would give us a rousing cheer on our way.

Very soon the heavy gradient slackened the speed which became a slow 'chooga-choog' towards the Calton Tunnel. Inside this cavern smoke from the leading engine was dense, the air humid. Conditions on the footplate were difficult with no clean air to breathe. But there was a flow of clean air at rail level so the thing go do was to ride on the lower footstep and breathe deeply.

As we emerged from the tunnel into the brightly lit Waverley station the night air flooded around us and we could clearly see the snake-like train running onto the Suburban line, the guard on his veranda ready with his shunting pole to unhook the J36. If he couldn't manage to do this from above he would ride on the brakevan step and uncouple from the side.

We didn't have to stand long in isolation before green signal lights traced a path towards the tunnel and back to Leith, free wheeling down the hill tender leading.

There was also need for assistance over the Lothian Lines, a single track from South Leith Junction to Niddrie West, and the Suburban line and to Wanton Walls and the East Coast route at Monktonhall Junction. This line was controlled by the 'Lock and Block' system using semaphore signals and relieved congestion in the Portobello area where the main line was crossed by a bridge in the vicinity of Portobello East Junction signalbox which straddled the main line. Trains being assisted over this lofty railway at night appeared like Vulcans chariots of fire in the sky.

Further round the Suburban railway at Duddingston two Class J35's stood ready to assist trains to Morningside Road. The enginemen were lodged in an ancient carriage body with coal fire central heating, cosy on a winters night. They had telephone communication with the signalmen who alerted them when assistance was required. If all these banking engines were in action at the same time at night there was a ring of fire around Edinburgh.

Chapter 26

Single Line Working

The Electric Token Block System on single lines was extensively used in Scotland and St Margarets men had a good share of this method of signalling on the Galashiels via Peebles line where there was about 10 token exchange points. This railway ran from the Waverley Route at Hardengreen Junction to south of the Pentland Hills and east of the Moorfoot Hills then down the valley of Eddleston Water, serving mill towns and agricultural industry.

There was rural beauty in abundance on this tortuous route but in darkness such delights were of no consequence. When I fired "Scotts" and "Glens" on the Galashiels via Peebles line in 1947 it was always in early morning darkness. In the cab there was firelight glare and the feeble light of a water gauge lamp beyond this there was only blackness punctured in places by isolated crofts and farms identified by dismal lantern. We sensed our progress and position by sounds like passing over bridges or hearing reverberation from some structure until ahead we could see the pale lights of a signalbox and station. This was the time to reduce speed to 10 mph as I prepared to exchange tablets.

The tablet took the form of a brass disc with two station names thereon and it was important these names applied to the section of line being passed over. This disc was in a stout leather pouch attached to a wide handle. I had to position myself firmly on the oscillating footplate and to do this I would press one knee against the tender structure and the other knee against the cab side. Then my arms were extended at different angles to my body, the left arm held high and forward the right arm directed low and holding tablet by the disc, the looped handle outstretched. Meanwhile, the signalman on his raised wooden stand would be preparing to deliver tablet held high in his right hand while his left hand was ready to receive tablet from me. This delicate manoeuvre required slow speed but in some places where automatic exchange apparatus was in use the changeover could be done at higher speed using a clip holder on side of cab delivering to a clip holder at signalbox.

This system was in use on the Highland railways in some places. I found however, manual effort prevailed the day I went to Dalguise working a special passenger train with a Class B1 engine. I had a conductor from Perth and soon we were beyond Stanley Junction and running at speed over the former Caledonian line to Inverness. While standing behind the Perth driver admiring the scenery I noticed tunnels and other structures were smaller than usual, then suddenly there was a loud bang close to my face, in catching the tablet the pouch had swung on the speeding engine's outside hitting it with a powerful slap.

In the immediate post war years St Margarets had 15 Class V1 2-6-2T and half a dozen Class C16 4-4-2T for Suburban work. But there was one local job, the 5.18 pm Waverley to Corstorphine, that was a train spotters delight. The first available passenger engine went on the '5.18' — Pacific, Green Arrow, K3, Shire, Scott, Glen, anything with wheels and an automatic brake. The passengers on this train were mostly railway office workers and the procedure on arrival at Corstorphine was to stop short of the buffer stop so that locomotive could round train. This meant a few yards extra walk for commuters and these people complained about this. Consequently an order went up at St Margarets instructing drivers to stop nearer the exit.

The return working for this train was booked to stop at all intermediate stations —! Pinkhill, Balgreen Halt, Haymarket. When I was on this cushy job one day the guard came to me and said "There are no passengers, Charlie, so if there are none at Pinkhill and Balgreen Halt just keep going", then as an afterthought he said, "you'd better stop at Haymarket — you never know who's watching".

Years later a driver at Thornton was called before the boss for failing to make a booked stop. "What's the good of stopping?" he said. "I knew there was nobody on the train and I could see there was nobody on the platform so I kept going". "Alright", said the boss, "but watch it in future".

Chapter 27

Accidents and Incidents

Though fondly remembered by many people the steam locomotive created problems not readily apparent. Under the Railway Fires Acts 1905 and 1923, railway companies are liable for damage to forests, woods, orchards, market and nursery gardens, agricultural land and fences, or crops, resulting from sparks from locomotives. It is essential for all railway employees to exercise the greatest vigilance at all times to prevent fires, and, where they occur, to extinguish them.

Although nowadays dependent on local authorities for fire fighting, British Railways used to have volunteer teams to combat fires at depots and yards, just as they have trained first aid personnel to deal with personal injuries, there were also fire officers trained in every aspect of the work whose function was mainly fire prevention. These were the people who ensured that fire appliances were properly serviced and maintained throughout the railway industry.

In steam days train fires were caused by sparks from the locomotive, over-heated journals and sometimes ammunition, the latter especially during the wars. With the steam locomotive there was no shortage of water for dousing a fire and a bucket was available for use in such an emergency. If a vehicle on the train was alight there was a definite drill laid down to isolate the fire. The 'heroic' trainmen would uncouple the blazing wagon which was moved forward and isolated from the rear of the train then uncoupled and separated from the front of the train, so that there was no danger of the fire spreading to other vehicles.

The demise of the steam locomotive greatly reduced the risk of such fires and the payment by railway companies of compensation in respect of same. The fitting of spark arresters to steam engines eliminated the problem to some extent. Ashes were drawn through a wire net screen and were small, dead and harmless when ejected through the chimney. That was the theoretical answer to the problem but in practise only modern steam engines had this fitment and the risk to the countryside remained serious enough for railway companies to include specific reference to lineside fires in the general appendix, listing 'danger zones' supplied by the Forestry Commission.

With diesel traction, the combination of oil spillage and heavy braking is the most common cause of train fires. Having a low flash-point, diesel oil tends to give off smoke rather than flame, but "where there's smoke there's fire", so it is still a serious problem.

Modern rail traction is less prone to structural defects than the steam locomotive, which was a spidery of nuts and bolts, every one with inherent weakness and liable to work loose or break apart. A contemporary of mine, Sandy Denholm, was driving home from Newcastle one morning when he heard an awful bang. He thought the engine had struck something and duly stopped at the first signalbox, Cragmill, where his mate signed the train register and reported the loud bang.

Meanwhile, with the feeble light of a small torch (all conscientious drivers provided themselves with these handy lights) Sandy examined the engine front to back but could find nothing damaged. Then he came again to the front of the engine and made to lean on the left buffer but it was not there! Its loss had been the bang.

There was also the occasion when a bogie wheel fell off a Pacific loco as it bumped its way across the table at Haymarket. Such defects were usually seen by the examiner during regular inspection but hairline fractures and other minute imperfections were sometimes missed under a layer of dirt. This mud could, however, reveal a crack which was perpetrated in the crust formed.

Accidents came easily in goods yards, the most common being rough shunts, damage to vehicles and contents. 'Tight crossings' were another hazard, for instance when insufficient clearance was left between vehicles on converging roads. Anyone riding on the locomotive footplate had to look out for this danger. Too often a man has been caught off guard with tragic consequences.

Over anxious firemen, guards, and shunters were always at risk as they prepared to couple up before the buffers met and many have died in the attempt.

Fly shunting was frowned on but acceptable in certain circumstances. This movement had the engine leading with wagons behind. There would be a man to control the hand-points and a shunter to uncouple the loco at the precise moment. A driver required plenty of room to do a fly shunt and had to exceed the speed of the trailing wagons as soon as the shunter had uncoupled. In this way the loco ran clear of the points while the pointsman re-set them to allow the wagons into another road. It was a risky manoeuvre not to be encouraged but a fly shunt never failed to give me a strange thrill, it reminded me of an errant schoolboy caught raiding an orchard and smartly avoiding a kick in the pants.

The derailment of a passenger train in the late 70's near Cowlairs was found to be caused by a slack tyre the securing part of which was later recovered in Haymarket tunnel at Edinburgh. To make it easier for examiners to detect such flaws before a train went into service it was decided to paint the wheels white. I seem to recall the expediency of this idea was recognised a very long time ago.

Though he does not dwell on it, a worrying possibility to a train driver is an obstruction on the opposite running line. Such an accident with which I am familiar happened at Longniddry Junction on 17th December 1953 and involved the Class A2 Pacific No 60530 'Sayajirao' with Haymarket men aboard.

It was near Christmas and the train left Waverley

station at 12.48 am, seven minutes later than its booked time, loaded with parcels for Kings Cross. The engine with its 8 wheeled tender weighed 161 tons in working order and its train comprised 9 bogie and 19 four wheeled vans weighing approximately 450 tons. 'Sayajirao' was in fine fettle in the able hands of Driver D. Drummond and Fireman R. McKenzie and she was soon gathering speed through the Edinburgh suburbs, past Monktonhall Junction and racing towards Prestonpans, at milepost 9½.

It was a cold, clear night and firebeam pierced the fleeting white clouds as it traced the course of the parcels express. Semaphore signals, all showing bright green aspects, swam into view as Prestonpans flashed by and the train raced on to Longniddry Junction. At this stage, 'Sayajirao' was doing what her designer Edward Thompson had intended, pulling her load at high speed. As if to reassure himself that maximum steam pressure was being made available Driver Drummond pulled on the already wide open throttle and checked the 'cut off' was right for economic use of the steam in the cylinders. The engine cab was aglow as Fireman McKenzie stopped shovelling coal and operated the water injector then edged on to his seat to enjoy the cool slip stream of the speeding train. The time was 1.18 am — the speed 60 m.p.h.

Suddenly, and without warning, the great Pacific loco hit an obstruction, stood momentarily on its nose, fell across the up platform at Longniddry Junction, then rolled down an embankment, coming to rest with its wheels in the air and facing towards Edinburgh. Fireman McKenzie was killed instantly and Driver Drummond seriously injured.

The obstruction was a 'decauville' track turn-out that had fallen on the up line from an open wagon of a down freight train which passed through the station just before the parcels train.

The up platform was demolished over a distance of 123 yards and the down platform damaged for 20 yards. A length of 147 yards of the up track including the trailing end of a crossover, was destroyed and the down track was distorted for about 70 yards.

The cause of this sad accident was the failure, due to chafing, of the rope securing the overhanging part of the load in the wagon of a freight train, the 9.45 pm Heaton to Edinburgh. Once the rope broke the manner in which it had been attached allowed the whole of it, and the load, to become loose. No centre rope had been affixed and consequently the top piece of the load was able to become displaced sufficiently to strike the column at Longniddry and be thrown on to the opposite line in the path of the parcels train.

The difference between safety and danger — life and death — is sometimes determined in a very short space of time, a few minutes, or perhaps seconds. It is as if fate had decreed that an accident should happen and rushes in at the crucial moment to make sure it does happen. Such was the case when an articulated lorry from Ulster left the A75 and attempted to cross a bridge over the Carlisle-Dumfries railway line.

It was a very tight manoeuvre for such a big vehicle with the result that it crashed onto the railway with its load of bottles right into the path of the overnight Euston to Stranraer sleeper train running fast under clear signals. The lorry was dragged for about a mile and its driver and locomotive crew were all killed.

Traffic is sparse on this railway and had the lorry taken a dive a few seconds later there would have been ample time to deal with the accident without hazarding a train.

Many railway bridges pass over water but sometimes the water passes over the bridges. When this happened on the East Coast route in 1948 between Berwick and Granthouse it was a catastrophe rather than an accident. Exceptionally heavy storms in south-east Scotland on August 11th and 12th were followed by floods which caused very severe damage in the valley of the Eye Water where seven railway bridges were swept away.

James Paterson of Haymarket depot was the driver of the last train through before complete closure of the line. For this valiant effort Jim received a certificate of merit from a grateful management, and this memento, suitably framed, adorned his sitting room wall.

Temporary military-type bridges were built to replace those swept away by the floods. They were erected in such a way that after the reopening of the line to traffic it would be possible to build concrete abutments and wing-walls as substructures for the permanent bridges without causing interference with traffic. The main line was opened within 12 weeks of the disaster — for goods traffic on October 25th, and for passengers on November 1st.

Among the secondary lines that suffered damage was the 3 mile branch from Burnmouth to Eyemouth which crossed the Eye Water at a height of 60 ft on a viaduct of 50 ft wrought-iron lattice-girded spans, supported on brick faced concrete piers. The centre pier was undermined by the scouring action of the flood, and collapsed, but the girders were not dislodged.

Railways, and particularly certain types of railway structures, are liable to suffer extensive damage from subsidence. Viaducts and, above all, tunnels were especially vulnerable, for while the lining of a tunnel, be it of brick or reinforced concrete or any other combination of materials, will serve to protect the tunnel against small local displacements of the adjoining rock, where it was weakened or shattered by blasting when the tunnel was being made, this lining cannot resist the enormous stresses which may be set up when a large mass perhaps several hundreds of metres in thickness settles down a few metres and becomes split and riven in the process. While in passage through Penmanshiel tunnel and other tunnels I sometimes marvelled at the effort and expertise that created them but never thought of the geological defects that could destroy them — just as well too!

Certain provisions of the Railway Clauses Consolidation Act of 1845 regularised the respective rights of a railway company and a mine owner with regard to the working of coal under or near a railway. These provisions which became known as the Mining Code, allowed a mine owner to work any minerals (including coal) under and

16. Four Pacifics illustrate the restricted space at St Margarets. From left to right: No 60024 "Kingfisher"; No 60052 "Prince Palatine"; No 60530 "Sayajirao"; No 60121 "Silurian". (N E Stead)

17. Class D49 No 306 "Roxburghshire" with cleaning squad at St Margarets 1936. (Author's collection)

18. Class A3 No 60099 "Call Boy" at Haymarket. Note the buckets on ground (with spouts) used for filling sand boxes located under boiler. It was precarious work standing on a narrow footplate beside splashers shaking sand into boxes.

19. Class D30 No 62429 "TheAbbot" at Thornton, its home for many years.

20. 0-6-0 3F Class J35 No 4478 out of breath on the Silloth line but within shouting distance of Carlisle Canal shed, its home.

21. 0-6-0 2F No 68477 the Waverley East pilot under the shadow of St Andrews House, formerly Calton Jail. The signal gantry supported semaphore signals and platform numbers before colour light signals came in 1938.

22. NBR 4-4-0 No 35 "Glen Gloy" brand new at Thornton in
1920. Driver Tommy Thomson with pourie on footplate
fronted by John Allan (Inspector); W Simpson (Running
Foreman); J Ellis (Loco Foreman).
The wee boy is John Allan's son.

23. St Margarets B1 No 61398 on the 4.10pm Edinburgh –
Hawick stops at Fountainhall on the Waverley route. Fitted
with electric headlamps (dynamo on footplate next to
smokebox) it is an oil lamp at chimney that indicates
stopping passenger train.

24. *NBR Atlantic No 9903 "Cock 'o the North" at No 9 platform, Waverley station with the St Margaret's breakdown crane on exhibition. This same engine hauled Field Marshall Earl Haig's funeral train to St Boswells in 1928. The name was transferred to Gresley Class P2 in 1934 and No 9903 became "Aberdonian". (A A McLean)*

25. *Gaffers line-up at St Margarets 1936. Left to right: Jock Innes: Bob Wright: Willie Kay: Nehemiah Knox: John Culver: Jimmy Nixon: Jimmy Brown.*

26. *St Margarets Class D34 No 62487 "Glen Arklet" departs from Bonnyrigg en route to Galashiels via Peebles. Note driver's hand on window frame as he gains purchase in opening steam regulator.*

27. *Class V2 No 60840 (Dundee Tay Bridge) working an express passenger is slowed by signals at Dalmeny on leaving the Forth Bridge.*

28. *St Margarets Class V3 No 67607 on suburban train between Craiglockart and Gorgie. This service was used for practical driving tests.*

29. *North Eastern Class R (LNER Class D20) introduced in 1899. They were built without superheaters, but all were later superheated. No 592 being turned manually at Haymarket.*

30. *Line-up at Dunfermline on a smokeless Sunday or Fife holiday. From left to right: Class WD 2-8-0 Nos 90019 and 90386: Class J38 No 65906: Class J36 tender.*

31. *Class D31 4-4-0 No 9770. One of these engines was stabled at Dunbar for assisting trains to Granthouse and other local work. The last of this class, No 62281, was withdrawn at Carlisle Canal in 1952 after working on the Silloth Branch. Note Class B12 in background with ACF1 feed water heater atop boiler giving rise to the name "hiker". It was also a hike for the fireman shovelling coal from the short 3-wheeled tender.*

within a lateral distance of forty yards from railway property without incurring any liability for damage by subsidence provided that he gave the railway company thirty days notice of his intentions, and that the coal was worked in a proper and customary way. As time passed and as the mining of coal went to depths which were not commonly thought of in 1845, the subsidence resulting from these deep workings resulted in special restrictions on adjacent railways.

At Thornton Junction in Fife some coal workings were so shallow that miners judged the time by the passage of trains. The speed of these trains was severely restricted because of the unstable nature of the ground. Station platforms were reconstructed a few times in the battle against subsidence and there are still houses at Thornton lying back at a crazy angle with people resident there.

Having been born in the shadow of the Forth Bridge, at Dalmeny, this place has held an interest for me over the years. This great structure has had few accidents considering its potential for same. To my knowledge there has only been one derailment, a train hauled by the engine 'Bantam Cock' during WW 2.

Over fifty men died and several hundred received injuries during the seven years the bridge was under construction. It was foreseen, therefore, that there could be problems with the maintenance of this massive structure, amongst other possibilities someone might "take a dive", that is, fall from the heights into the cold waters of the River Forth.

As a precaution against such accidents proving fatal it was arranged for a wee boat to be in position below the bridge during normal working hours with two men aboard to deal with rescue operations. This small craft was kept in the tranquil harbour at South Queensferry and went to its anchorage near the bridge every morning of every working day, returning to harbour in the late afternoon.

The crew was very rarely called upon to effect a rescue so to pass the time they would develop a simple hobby, fishing being the most popular. Then there was the chance to take a walk on Inch Garvie the small island which supports the middle structure of the bridge where many 'lucky' pennies landed. Today, there is a joint rescue service for the two bridges spanning the river at Queensferry and those lazy boating days are but a memory.

During my childhood at Dalmeny a locomotive fireman was killed on the Forth Bridge when he climbed over the engine tender and was struck by the granite hardness of the south portal. In more recent times, however, the accident I readily recall involved a very lucky passenger on a north-bound train.

It was a very dark Saturday night when the last train from Edinburgh sped towards Dalmeny and the south approach viaduct. A man on the train must have expected the train to stop and seemed unaware of its speed. He opened a door, alighted on what he thought was the station platform but it turned out to be the stone parapet of the viaduct. After bouncing from this solid structure he fell about 50 feet into a small woodland where trees cushioned his landing. The guard stopped the train and alerted the emergency services and the unfortunate 'high diver' was taken back to Edinburgh — to hospital.

Only slightly less unnerving was the experience of Thornton men working a freight train over the Forth Bridge more than 150 feet above high water level. After inspection at Dalmeny the train proceeded onto the bridge with the driver at the controls and the fireman shovelling coal. Laying down the shovel he climbed onto his 'perch', a piece of wood hinged to the cab side — one could hardly call it a seat. It was a beautiful night with a full moon illuminating the intricate girder work of the great cantilevers astride the Forth. Soft white puffs from the engine chimney quickly dissipated as cool breezes swept them through the entanglement of steel. In the canopy of the sky white clouds remained permanent and the dark waters far below reflected the lunar margin that enlivened the whole estuary.

As the fireman marvelled at the glory of the night he was suddenly aware of an interruption in the ribbons of steel upon which the train ran, it appeared as a great gap, an ominous darkness.

"Stop, mate" the fireman yelled, "the bridge is down!" All the horror of that disastrous December night in 1879 when the Tay Bridge collapsed was vivid to the Thornton driver as he wrestled to control the momentum of his goods train, slamming on the steam brake and quickly reversing the motions. The startled fireman, too, got into the act as he screwed tight the tender brake.

With sparks flying, rotating wheels changed direction and four strong exhaust beats gave way to violent contractions as the changed position of the valve gearing affected the passage of steam. Suddenly, all was still with only the echoing sound of lengthening couplings disturbing the new found peace as the train adjusted itself to a stationary position yards from the gaping hole.

But, there was no hole. As the enginemen stared at what had threatened their survival and tested their nerves they realised the black 'abyss' was in fact a wagon sheet that had come off a train and covered part of the railway which the moon had revealed in stark relief. No doubt it was 'stark relief', too, for those Thornton men to learn the truth.

During my lifetime I have travelled on land, sea and in the air on a variety of conveyances but none were more exciting and exhilarating than a steam engine. Notable in my experience is the vibrating, cake-walk effect in the cab of a Class J37 as this 0-6-0 raged with a 1 in 70 incline on the Waverley Route trailing empty bucking coal wagons for Lady Victoria Pit.

Another experience to inflame the spirit was driving a dilapidated V2 with an express freight train on the East Coast at night. Every steam joint and piston gland would be blowing to unite with the chimney exhaust in a cacophony of hissing harshness as hot cinders bounced on the track and shot over the engine, like tracer bullets.

Ghosts at St Margarets......

I'm standing beside a railway gate
On a slope called "Smokey Brae"
Accompanied by a withered mate
Far gone in bone decay
This used to be our working place
How I remember well
My empty frame I try to brace
Emotion is hard to quell
No longer does the smoke ascend
Shrouding the Royal Park
No locomotives here to tend
With fire-glow in the dark
Men who laboured in the yards
Have long ago passed on
Drivers, firemen and guards
Gaffers, too, have gone

Firedroppers, boilermen
Fitters making joints
Office clerks with all the gen
Trackmen oiling points
The signalbox is now no more
No shining levers to pull
Where once there was a semaphore
Electric signals rule

Gone is the worry and the care
The need to get things done
Now, in unpolluted air

Intimacy with the sun
Gone forever the railway track
Gone with the running shed
No sad regret in thinking back
You see, we, too, are dead.

**The Waverley Route
A Trilogy**
(First published by Cheviot Publications, Hawick
and edited by Bill Peacock)

Disaster on a Waverley Route Train

Five years after the event, the railway accident near Carlisle Canal Junction on January 3rd, 1931, was still a topic of conversation amongst the Carlisle railway fraternity which I joined temporarily in 1936.

I remember my landlady, Mrs Rae, talking about the Pullman train from Edinburgh that had "become a cropper" only yards from its destination. In sad reflection she would lower her head and, through trembling lips, mutter "poor Jack, poor Jack Eskdale." This was a sincere expression of sympathy from the heart of an engine driver's wife. "Sal", as her man called her, was the "better half" of Carlisle Canal's popular Jock Rae whose brother, Bill, was permanent way inspector at Langholm. She had fierce pride in railways and was truly distressed by the tragedy of "poor Jack Eskdale", the driver of the ill-fated 12 noon Pullman train from Edinburgh to London St Pancras via Hawick and Carlisle.

Fate is the power by which things are predetermined. It is our destiny, our lot, and we have no control over it. So it was with Jack Eskdale, senior "spare" driver at St Margarets depot in Edinburgh. Circumstances on January 3rd, 1931, caused him to take over the duties of driver Willie Meiklejohn who was on leave. Jack found himself rostered with another "spare" man, Fireman John Wardle, to work the 12 noon to Carlisle via Hawick.

It was a fine but cold day, ideal for human effort on a

steam engine. Their charge was the D49 "Shire" class locomotive "Northumberland". To a "spare" driver, the prospect of working a "top link" express passenger train brought mixed feelings of apprehension and elation. There was some anxiety about route knowledge, timing and fast running. At forty-nine years of age, Jack Eskdale had a great deal of footplate experience, but shunting engines, coal trains and fast freight workings were far less demanding than express passenger jobs. These were second nature to Willie Meiklejohn and other "top link" drivers, but a real test for "spare" crewmen. Any misgivings, however, usually gave way to exultation at the thought of improved status and higher earnings.

At thirty years of age, John Wardle was considered to be an experienced fireman and had worked with Meiklejohn the previous day. He had been passed for this work in 1917.

The locomotive "Northumberland" was built in 1929 and came to St Margarets in April of that year so she was barely two years old. Up to the date of the accident, the engine had run 81,777 miles and had given little or no trouble. It seemed the locomotive could not be faulted, but would the ability of the "spare" crewmen match such apparent perfection? They were destined to be put to the test that day.

The tortuous Waverley Route terrain was a constant challenge to the most experienced enginemen, although a long, practical acquaintance with this road was a great advantage. Familiarity with locomotives and their indivi-dual temperament was also important, along with the driver's own self-assurance and confidence in his fireman. This was the desired state of affairs but it was not always that way in practice, while other factors including poor quality coal often influenced the situation.

Jack Eskdale stood proudly in the cab of "Northumber-land" as she ran tender first uphill from St Margarets to the narrow confines of Waverley Station. There, at platform one, the "Shire" was coupled to a train of seven vehicles weighing a total of 210 tons. This was forty tons below the authorised maximum load for a "Shire" engine working the Waverley Route.

Guard David Scott was in charge of the train and exchanged notes with Driver Eskdale regarding the weight, number of vehicles and booked stops. He was a man of fifty years of age with twenty-six years service, eighteen of which were as a passenger guard. This long experience seemed an advantage over Driver Eskdale but the real measure of a railwayman's ability is proper use of such working knowledge, to anticipate danger and protect his train.

As usual, the 12 noon Carlisle train had a near capacity load that fateful day, and the dining car staff of a cook and two attendants worked hard to satisfy the demand for food and refreshments. The train left Edinburgh on time with Guard Scott riding in the fifth vehicle and the engine crew determined to at least equal the performance of the "professionals", Messrs Meiklejohn and company.

The "Shire" proved sprightly on the run to Hardengreen but the rising gradient to Falahill and poor quality coal resulted in a loss of five minutes. Once over the summit, the run down Falahill bank was made at the booked speed of fifty-two miles per hour. another three minutes were lost while taking water at Galashiels, but the run to Hawick, with stops at Melrose and St Boswells, was made without falling further behind. However, another minute was lost at Hawick where some 200 passengers detrained, and the express was nine minutes in arrears leaving there. The long, steep climb to Whitrope Summit caused a loss of another two minutes and the train was eleven minutes late by the time Riccarton Junction was reached. This was according to the Riccarton signalman's record, but Eskdale later said he had looked at his watch while passing the Junction and noted he wasnine minutes behind time.

Subsequently, Guard Scott, in his evidence, said: "From Whitrope to Newcastleton, we recovered one minute, and two minutes from Newcastleton to passing Longtown Junction, where we were seven minutes late." Scott added: "The driver was running hard from Riccarton Junction down the bank, but especially from Newcastleton. He was running much harder in my opinion than the regular man (Meiklejohn). I could not call the speed alarming on the straight, flat road, but it was much faster than usual, that is between Newcastleton and Canal Junction. I think he was going between fifty and sixty miles per hour."

Eskdale could have been doing what every driver was expected to do in trying to make up lost time, with due regard to safety and speed limits. In the actions of a "spare" man there could, however, have been a tendency to disregard point-to-point timings, despite the best intentions. There was nothing in Guard Scott's evidence to show that Eskdale was acting irresponsibly although it seems unlikely that a speed restriction of fifty miles per hour at Longtown was strictly adhered to, and still less likely that speed through Harker was as low as thirty miles per hour.

Eskdale maintained that when he approached Canal Junction at thirty miles per hour after crossing the London — Glasgow main line at Kingmoor, he observed the distant signal in the clear position, by which he knew he had an unrestricted run to No 3 box. He closed the regulator while passing over the level crossing, 1020 yards from Canal Junction box. He returned the reversing lever to full forward position and began to apply the brake, vacuum being reduced from twenty-one inches to ten inches. He said this "reduced speed rapidly" and estimated that Canal Junction box was passed at fifteen miles per hour. He also said that while maintaining about ten inches of vacuum, speed was the same entering the curve after passing No 1 box.

Evidently, however, the accident occurred without warning of any kind. Eskdale's words were: "All of a sudden, I had a sensation that the engine suddenly stopped, my tea bottle fell off the shelf and my fireman was thrown over my right arm. Immediately after that, I had a sinking feeling as if I was in a descending lift, this was before the engine left the rails. I am positive of that. I did not feel anything at all — it just rolled over."

Although Fireman Wardle had been told the previous day by Meiklejohn of the need to reduce speed on the two curves concerned, he was too busy with the fire to afford guidance to Eskdale.

Guard Scott, for his part, made a belated move to apply his brake, so his experience as a passenger guard counted for little.

The facts were that the train left the rails on a right handed curve between Nos 1 and 3 signal boxes at Carlisle. The engine turned over on its left side on an ashtip that had been formed adjacent to the line. The busy London Midland Scottish main line was blocked as a result of the derailment, causing serious disruption to the London Euston — Glasgow services.

It was fortunate that 200 passengers had left the doomed train at Hawick and only about 40 remained when the accident occurred, the majority being in the leading coaches. Three people were killed and many injured, including the train crew.

It is interesting to speculate why Eskdale failed to properly control his train, although his own evidence does not admit such a lapse. He must have signed the Route Book and confirmed his knowledge of the Edinburgh-Hawick-Carlisle line, otherwise he would not have been rostered to replace Meiklejohn.

Sometimes, a driver's concentration can be affected when "idle thoughts" enter his head, but Eskdale, in his evidence, left no room for such human failings. It is more likely that his inexperience over that particular part of the route deprived him of the full knowledge the job demanded. If only someone at St Margarets or elsewhere had mentioned the need for extra care on the approach to Carlisle Citadel station, if only Meiklejohn had been at the controls, if only........

The evidence of signalmen and other observers left no doubt that speed had been excessive. As a result of the coroner's inquest on the deceased passengers at which the verdict of manslaughter against the driver was returned, Eskdale was committed for trial at the Cumberland Assizes at Carlisle. On June 3rd, 1931, he was found not guilty and acquitted.

As one who had experience of being a "spare" driver, elated for a day to take on an express passenger working, I can only echo the sentiments of long ago, those sad words from Mrs Rae: "Poor Jack, poor Jack Eskdale."

From this terrible accident, however, a lesson was learned and it was decided that distant signals on the approach to the accident site would in future be kept at caution.

When I last heard of Jack Eskdale he was on shunting duties at South Leith during World War 2.

"Flamingo" on the St. Pancras Sleeper

I first became acquainted with Sir Nigel Gresley's superbly designed A3 Pacific Locomotives when I joined the London and North Eastern Railway Company in March 1935. "Brown Jack", "Hyperion", "Windsor Lad" and others were standing at Edinburgh's Haymarket shed to greet me. However, it was at Carlisle Canal depot in 1936 that I became closely involved with these engines as one of my regular duties was cleaning "Captain Cuttle", "Colorado" and "Flamingo", the three race-horses whose Derby techniques had to adapt to the Grand National challenge of the Waverley Route.

At that time, Carlisle Canal crews worked the "Thames-Forth" express to Edinburgh via Hawick, returning over the same route with the sleeper train for London St Pancras. On arrival at Edinburgh Waverley, the engine was uncoupled and proceeded to St Margarets depot via Lochend and Piershill Junctions, turning itself in the process. Carlisle men serviced their own engines, then usually stopped to drink stewed tea from a glass bottle and ate their "bait" (snack), the Cumbrian equivalent of the Scottish "piece"!

Before leaving St Margarets shed, there was time to make up the fire and have a chat with anyone so inclined. I worked at St Margarets for twenty-seven years and, knowing the Carlisle men from my Canal days, I often used to have a blether with them. One evening, I recall being in the company of Fred Graham and Bobby Borrowdale, characters you would never encounter on today's railways. Their distinctive qualities and traits had developed according to the testing demands of the steam locomotives in their charge. Fred was big and stout with white hair crowning a ruddy complexion. This "John Bull" driver was always cracking jokes and shaking with his own laughter, just one of many memorable characters I encountered during my railway service.

Although there were numerous other trains on the Waverley Route, I particularly remember the "Thames-Forth" and St Pancras sleeper services. I used the former regularly on my many visits to "Bronte Land" from where my wife originated. On the return north, we would join the train at Keighley then, in later times, at Skipton.

During the 1930's, the night train to St Pancras was my means of getting back to Carlisle after a weekend in Edinburgh. It was also the service that took me to war in 1940 when I joined the Royal Engineers at Derby, but most of all, I remember it for a ride on the footplate of A3 Pacific "Flamingo" when I was a cleaner laddie at Canal shed.

The landlord of my Carlisle digs was Jock Rae, an engine driver, and he used to say: "if ever I'm on that Edinburgh job when you're on the train, I'll have you up front with me!" This "threat" was never taken seriously until one night at Edinburgh Waverley as I settled with my workmates in a cosy compartment, I heard a knock on the window and there was Jock, grinning and beckoning me to join him on the footplate. I was wearing a blue serge suit and white shirt but the coal dust that lay in store did not deter me — I had the opportunity to experience what had long been a distant dream.

"Flamingo" looked magnificent as she simmered in the shadows of Waverley Station, her shining boiler reflecting the platform lights as steam and smoke blended with the night. To me, she represented more than an image of dynamic energy which heat and water had created. I had also known her in more gentle mood on shed, wiping grime from her apple green coat and burrowing and cleaning deep inside her belly. I knew something about her and now I was to see her perform.

There is nothing quite like the cab of a live steam locomotive, especially one of "Flamingo's" calibre. Darkness seems to emphasise the warmth and distinctive fragrance of an oil and steam mixture. Above the fireglow, the driver and fireman became part of the shadows, only their legs clearly showing. On Gresley Pacifics, the driver had a swivel shield to protect his legs from the intense heat, but this was denied the fireman, probably because he had no time to sit down, such was the incessant demand for coal. This is just how it was on the steeply graded Waverley Route with little opportunity for idling by the stoker. Because he was thus engaged, I was assured a seat all the way to Carlisle and was grateful for the secure corner.

Sitting there at Waverley, I felt I was intruding on the Fireman's space but this good man very soon put me at ease. I felt even more part of the team when Jock called out: "How's that, Charlie?" He was referring to the starting signal which had changed from red to green, and, with the fireman's backing, I responded: "Right away, Jock".

In those days, the signals at Waverley East were a battery of semaphores but the appropriate ones were easily identified at night, the green lights contrasting clearly with the red lamps. There was also less chance of conflicting movements because at 9.50 pm when the St Pancras sleeper left, the shunting crews were changing shifts.

On confirming the signal position, Jock pulled strongly on the dual-handled steam regulator, quickly closing it again as the A3 Pacific took the strain of shifting nine carriages weighing in excess of 300 tons. Just as quickly, steam was re-applied and as "Flamingo's" nose dipped towards Calton Tunnel, strain gave way to relaxed momentum. the fireman was also instinctively carrying out his duties and glanced back at the flickering lights of the snake-like train as it negotiated the twisting exit from the station. In Calton Tunnel, partial darkness in the cab gave way to a flood of light from the fire, while Jock's grin conveyed the satisfaction he felt at having got me "up front". My offer of a seat to the fireman was declined with a wave of his hand as he shouted above the noise: "There's no time for sitting on this job — you wait and see!"

Flanked by lighted tenements, "Flamingo" pounded her way over the falling gradient, leaving in her wake drifting smoke and steam. Passing St Margarets, speed was restricted to thirty-five miles an hour and her potential remained under check until clear of Edinburgh's suburbs.

At Portobello East, where we diverted from the Edinburgh — Berwick — Newcastle route, speed was down to thirty miles an hour, while the stretch from Hardengreen Junction to Falahill Summit would present a prevailing rise of about 1 in 70 for nine miles.

Once clear of Niddrie South, the fireman began to demonstrate his expertise with left hand firing, facing the driver. His feet were anchored on the engine floorboards, clear of the swaying tender. His waist became a fulcrum as his strong arms carried each shovelful of coal from tender to the fire. It was a deliberate motion, well under control, directing the fuel to particular parts of the huge grate, measuring more than forty-one square feet.

"Flamingo's" six exhaust beats became more audible as she faced up to the challenge of Falahill. I felt far away from the passengers travelling behind us. Mine was a world of heat, noise and great activity, with excitement of the kind that made every boy want to become an engine driver.

Travelling through the dark countryside, there were occasional flickers of light where people lived in near isolation. Sounds were continually changing as we passed through gulleys, under and over bridges, and heard the locomotives voice reverberating across the hills. Now, we were approaching Falahill Summit, 880 feet above sea level, and the fireman laid down the shovel. Quickly I offered him his seat but he pushed me back on and shouted: "Stay where you are, Charlie, hold on — this is where we start to roll".

At the Summit, I caught a fleeting glimpse of the signalman waving us on our way, something unknown on railways nowadays. Jock consulted his watch and grinned contentedly as he shouted: "We're doing alright, Charlie".

"Flamingo's strong beats gave way to less distinct synchronised puffs as speed increased. It was "peaceful" enough to have a near normal conversation with me sitting tight and the fireman gripping the back of the seat. "That's the fire cleaned, Charlie, up the chimney with it. I'll start shovelling again at Gala", said the cheerful stoker.

Jock's head was out of the window watching for distant signals at Heriot, Fountainhall, Stow and Bowland. "It's easier to see signals on a clear night", said the fireman. "They seem to swim towards the driver whereas, during the day, you have to identify against a particular setting, look for a landmark and eventually spot the signal".

I noticed, too, that my conception of speed was also disturbed in the dark. I knew we were travelling fast but judgement was difficult unless measured against some object at the lineside and there were few indicators to be seen in the headlong dash through the dark night. The experienced enginemen could navigate blindly, it seemed, so I left it to the Carlisle men and gripped "Flamingo" tightly.

Soon after, Galashiels reflected in the night sky ahead and Jock braked for the ten miles an hour speed restriction approaching that station. The stop at Galashiels was brief but presented an opportunity for the fireman to shovel coal in comfort, and this he did, more purposeful than ever. As the black fuel hit the white-hot fire, smoke jets shot into the air from "Flamingo's" squat chimney. Spillage was swept up and the floor and coal regularly watered to keep down dust.

Most of the "sleeping" on the St Pancras sleeper train was actually done on Third Class compartment seats as there were only a few berths available for the real thing — nothing to compare with the night services on the East and West Coast Routes. It was a long, slow haul to St Pancras, lasting ten or eleven hours and over tortuous terrain with many stops. Galashiels was the first going southbound, followed in quick succession by Melrose, St Boswells and Hawick, so the night express had basically become a local stopping train. Passengers at these intermediate stations were few, and most of them alighted rather than boarded the train. "Flamingo's" style was somewhat cramped having to stop so often, but between stations the near level track was suitable for good bursts of speed.

Hawick, fifty-three miles from Edinburgh, was roughly half-way mark on theWaverley Route and where thirsty engines took on water as drivers checked for hot axle boxes or other mechanical defects. The fireman also had an opportunity to prepare for the stiff climb to Whitrope Summit, ten miles south and 1,006 feet above sea level with a maximum gradient of 1 in 72. Hawick was in slumberland as we ground to a halt on the curved platform, the time being 11.20 pm. As I watched the Carlisle men "fettling" their engine, I realised they had already completed a day's work and still had a long way to go. Hawick engine shed, in a hollow nearby, lay under a black cloud as smoke from old North British engines filled the air and drifted over our train.

Top link drivers on the Waverley Route would think twice before taking assistance for the climbs to Falahill and Whitrope, the assisting engine sometimes being more of a handicap than the incline itself. Nevertheless, it was prudent for southbound drivers to accept a push out of Hawick, sufficient to take them clear of the town, and that night "Flamingo's" wheels turned firmly with a wee engine pushing at the rear.

As we moved smartly into the Cheviot foothills, the lights of Hawick sparkled in the valley below. The blasting sound of the engine working hard would be an assurance rather than an annoyance to the sleeping Borderers. One gets used to the sound of trains when living in proximity to the tracks and the Border Union Railway had come to these parts in 1862.

The assisting engine soon left us to get on with it and Jock Rae set the controls for the best possible performance. After climbing through isolated Whitrope Tunnel, Jock waved to the signalman in the Summit box, then consulted his gold watch which momentarily sparked in the firelight — the time was 11.40 pm.

Speed began to build up and after clearing a forty miles an hour restriction at the sharp curve north of Riccarton Junction, "Flamingo" really took off.

I held on grimly as we raced down gradients to 1 in 72, through darkness that shrouded barren moors. From Newcastleton, the line was undulating to Penton then fell for three miles at 1 in 100 to Riddings Junction. Although Jock looked at his watch and patted the steam regulator handle occasionally, it was evident all was well.

After Canal Junction, the Pacific was more subdued as we moved over the double curve heading to Carlisle Citadel station. I could see the bright lights of Carrs Biscuit Works — "birthplace of the biscuit industry", and knew I was home again. That's how warmly I felt about Carlisle and the Rae family.

When "Flamingo's" wheels stopped turning, the Citadel clock showed 12.24 am. When I got down from the footplate, Jock was leaning over the cab window grinning.

"Thanks, Jock", I said, "I really enjoyed that!" He laughed and replied: "I knew you would. See you at the house!"

As I joined my mates leaving the train for the long walk to our digs, they too were laughing. But I didn't see the joke until I reached the house and looked in a mirror — I was as black as "Flamingo's" smoke box!

Atlantic Swell on the Waverley Route

The history of the Waverley Route is well documented and a clear picture emerges of a heavily graded railway where steam traction was worked to its limits. Having participated in this "engine bashing", I can only say the picture is not untrue, but there was more to this picturesque transport artery than sluggish goods trains, black smoke and clanging buffers.

When I moved from glamorous Haymarket locomotive shed at the west end of Edinburgh, to St Margarets depot in "Auld Reekie's" east end, I discovered that it was a midden which literally reeked to high heaven — reek from a varied selection of old North British Railway engines! It was 1936 and St Margarets engines and men, together with the ex-NBR depot at Carlisle Canal, monopolised the Waverley Route workings, although Polmont often provided an immaculate K3, No 181. The Carlisle men would set off on their long book-off trips to Edinburgh, Thornton and Dundee, while the "Jocks" worked similar jobs south to the old NBR outpost at Carlisle.

Although ex-Caledonian and North British men were distinguishable by their caps, they could also be recognised by other means. Whereas the Carlisle Kingmoor "Caley" men went booking-off with everything but the kitchen sink, the North British stalwarts from Canal shed journeyed north with only a piece box and a bottle of tea kept warm by the engine boiler!

But in 1936 it was not all drudgery on the Waverley Route — there was glamour too, and fast running! Previously, I was a telephone boy at Haymarket and saw at first hand the magnificent A4 and P2 locomotives designed by Sir Nigel Gresley. These were confined to the main East Coast route via Berwick and it seemed the St Margarets drivers would see nothing of this magic. They did, however, have one train to drive with pride — the 12.10 pm Edinburgh to Carlisle express via the Waverley Route.

For this glamour train, complete with Pullman restaurant car, we always cleaned and prepared one of the famous Atlantic engines designed by William Paton Reid. As locomotive cleaners, we were not immune to glamour and these massive engines were something special. To this day, I still recall how I enjoyed cleaning the smooth, curved footplate at the fore-end.

The men who fired these locomotives had served a long apprenticeship when promotion during the twenties and thirties was virtually non-existent. They had to be good at their job because as well as having to meet a continuous demand for steam, the rolling, bucking Atlantics often threatened to throw the stoker overboard at high speed. The driver was a bit more secure, wedged between the reversing lever and cab side! With names such as "Abbotsford", "Borderer", Buccleuch", Hazeldean", "Liddlesdale", "Teribus", and "Tweeddale", they became synonymous with the Borderland. Their shining steel rods surmounted by a powerful boiler and squat chimney, lent splendour to the sparkling paintwork.

Here, I recount a typical journey of this period on the 12.10 pm service, a train which undoubtedly enhanced the appearance of Waverley Station and the Waverley Route.

Coal was stacked high within a ribbed cage on the tender, providing a veritable mountain of work for one man. As starting time approached, the fireman controlled steam pressure with cooling water through the injector. Most of the hot coal was heaped just inside the firedoor on a ledge, a nucleus of intense heat which sustained the engine on its long haul south. The sloping firegrate was usually covered with glowing red cinders fanned by the air below. Once under way, a "light and often" shovelling technique ensured a thicker grate covering for the harsh Atlantic exhaust to bite on.

Meanwhile, passengers were settling into their comfortable compartments and seats. At the door of the Pullman restaurant car, the conductor, Bert Gillon, was welcoming his passengers aboard. His assistant, John Meacher (my brother), ushered them to their seats and generally saw to their comfort, while in the kitchen, Jean Stoddart, the only female cook I ever encountered on the railways, was busy preparing food.

The train had seven vestibule coaches with the Pullman car in the middle, weighing a total of 210 tons, the Atlantic's maximum load being 240 tons.

With the clock on the North British Hotel showing ten past twelve, the driver pulled on the whistle and the Waverley Route glamour train moved away towards Calton Tunnel, building up momentum on the falling gradient. The "spiders web" of rail crossings which had to be negotiated here gave the crew an early taste of the Atlantic's "rock and roll" capabilities, but the lurching subsided on the straight rails ahead.

The pace was increasing as Abbeyhill Junction came and went but on passing the thirty-five mile-an-hour restriction through St Margarets, the appearance of the Atlantic engine brought an acknowledging wave from the shed workers who knew her so well. The curved headboard below the chimney said it all — "Carlisle" — and there was the fireman sitting as if on a horse, lashing the cab side with the water spray pipe, like a jockey using a whip. this was just a lighthearted prelude to some hard work ahead and, almost immediately, the fireman took up the shovel to start feeding the engine's seemingly insatiable hunger, while the driver pulled on the whistle with one long and two short blasts, informing the signalman that the train was heading for the Carlisle line at Portobello East.

Speed was still restrained but once clear of the Portobello junction, the valve lever was pulled back a couple of notches and the steam regulator opened wide. Simultaneously, the fireman put on a spurt to keep up with the Atlantic's increased labouring as the train passed Niddrie North, Niddrie South, through Millerhill, on to the gentle slopes at Hardengreen and over the great Lothian Viaduct near Newtongrange.

On the hard climb to the 880 foot summit at Falahill, it was often one-handed firing on the Atlantics. After gathering a shovelful of coal, this was deftly laid on the firedoor frame, the ratchet doors opened with the right hand and the coal pushed forward with the left. Sometimes a helpful driver would operate the doors to make the firing task a little easier for his mate.

As the Atlantic revelled in the hill climbing so suited to

its rugged structure, life was more peaceful in the train itself. Attendant Meacher had advised passengers in every compartment that lunch was being served with the announcement: "Sittings for lunch, please". Bert Gillon had abandoned his paperwork to give personal attention to his clients, while Jean Stoddart worked even harder in her kitchen.

The travelling businessmen, farmers and ladies of leisure had little idea of the effort being expended on the locomotive footplate to get them to their destination. While the Atlantic barked towards Falahill Summit, they enjoyed the service for which the Pullman Car Company had become famous. Enjoyable food and refreshment were enhanced by the comfort of the carriage and the splendid panorama passing on either side.

From the engine cab, the view was equally impressive but there was no comfort on the rolling, swaying Atlantic. Food was usually a bite of cheese and toast, washed down with boiled tea from an overheated whisky bottle! At least on the descent to Galashiels there was time for relaxation, a chance to replenish the boiler and let the fire burn down.

Running swiftly downhill could be a nerve-wracking experience on these engines, the effect being reminiscent of the "cake-walk" as driver and fireman were bounced about on their seats. Heriot, Fountainhall, Stow and Bowland all flashed past, clear signals beckoning the express on. Back in the restaurant car, the diners were well into their second course.

Only slight use had been made of the vacuum brake on the twisting descent to Galashiels. Although the hills were a deterrent to sustained high speeds on the Waverley Route, station stops became a hindrance at places where increased speed was possible. On the approach to Galashiels, the driver gently operated the brake handle, his expertise ensuring a smooth "passenger stop".

As the wheels stopped turning, Bert Gillon stepped down to the platform his sparkling uniform resplendent in gold braid and buttons. Jean gave a quick look from her kitchen and, through the restaurant car window, attendant

Meacher could be seen clearing away the dishes in preparation for another sitting.

Galashiels was a hive of activity, station staff and passengers darting about in orderly confusion; parcels, barrows and milk cans in transit, people just standing watching.

On the Atlantic, the injector was "singing" as the fireman shovelled more coal through the firebox door. Eager to be on the move again, the driver impatiently viewed the starting signal ahead then looked back for the guard's green flag and the sound of the whistle. His reaction was instant when the "off" was given — the swift opening of the steam regulator, sending the driving wheels into a spin which he smartly checked, but not before leaving a black cloud rising above Gala.

From here to Hawick, only short bursts of speed were possible because of the closeness of the intermediate stations, although the relatively flat terrain lent itself well to rail traction.

St Boswells was only three miles away or a "long shunt" as some railwaymen would say. Although far from being an industrial centre, this interchange station serving Kelso, Jedburgh, Earlston, Duns and Berwick belied its rural appearance, with several small engines shedded there to work the branch trains. Although Galashiels was a larger place with branches to Selkirk and Peebles, the compact nature of St Boswells station, when complemented by the presence of a main-line train, tended to create the impression of a city terminal. For fleeting seconds with Bert Gillon and his Pullman car in the picture, it could well have been the setting for an Orient Express episode!

Water was available at St Boswells but with reasonable care and good fortune, the 4,240 gallons in an Atlantic tender were sufficient to reach Hawick, half-way mark on the ninety-eight and a quarter mile journey to "the birthplace of the biscuit industry" as Carrs of Carlisle used to advertise their town. With a brief salute to workmen at St Boswells locomotive shed, the crew prepared for the eight miles to Hawick. This stretch was the longest section of near level running the Atlantic had encountered since leaving Edinburgh. The pleasant wayside halts of Belses and Hassendean flashed past in quick succession.

Entering Hawick station on the sharply curved, canted track, passing crews could almost look down the chimneys of locomotives stabled at the large engine shed on the right. Here stood many veteran NBR engines including Scotts and Glens, while there was often an "intruder" from Newcastle which had journeyed over the Border Counties line via Hexham, Kielder and Riccarton. Being the largest town in the Borders, there was always great activity at Hawick and through trains lingered a little longer than at other stations en route. There was a lot of mail and parcel handling as well as the interchange of passengers. This gave the engine crew a chance to "fettle up" the Atlantic, take on water, check for overheating bearings, make up the fire and shovel the coal forward from the rear of the tender. There was little opportunity to study sheep in Oliver's auction mart at the foot of the embankment (the oldest livestock auctioneering firm in Britain, established in 1817), but there was adequate time for an experienced crew to do what was necessary. The Pullman car staff also took their chance to prepare for a final sitting.

The 1 in 75 gradient out of Hawick made starting difficult and some drivers called for assistance from the station pilot. Getting a push out of the "up" platform was a useful start on the long climb to Whitrope and Hawick men were always more than ready to help trains on their way.

The Waverley Route was a "doddle" to efficient engines and men, and in the 1930s, the St Margarets drivers had good status and were respected for their worth. They were normally allocated their own engines to nurse and cherish and no machine was better cared for or more intimately known. The driver who knew what his engine was capable of was not afraid of the Border hills.

This was so when the Atlantic tackled the steep gradient out of Hawick. With the lever in forward gear and the regulator just short of wide open, the great driving wheels turned firmly as they gripped the sand filtering on to the shining rails. If attentive, passengers would note the scenery passing less quickly and they might hear the sustained soft blasts of the hard working engine as the train climbed towards Whitrope.

Before long, the Atlantic blasted into the darkness of Whitrope Tunnel where the crew were engulfed in a crescendo of sound as the exhaust hit the roof. Then it was back out into the fresh air again and over the 1,006 feet summit where the lonely signalman was ready with a friendly wave, having played his part in passing the train safely on its way. Conscientiously, he stood at the window to view the train tail lamp and see that all was well.

Carlisle was still more than thirty miles away but the enginemen knew the worst was over. The fireman busied himself tidying up the cab and washing away the dust before anchoring himself to his seat. The driver was well prepared for the impending dash through Riccarton and a fast descent past lonely Steele Road. High speed eats up the mileage but booked stops at Newcastleton and Longtown spoiled what used to be a long fast run for this train. However, from Longtown to Carlisle Canal Junction was about nine miles of level track and an invitation for a final burst of speed. Nevertheless, the pace had to be restricted on the distant approach to Citadel station where the severe curvature of the line was a constant reminder of a bad incident there in 1931 when a Waverley Route train was derailed and three people killed. This accident, which is covered in detail elsewhere, served as a lesson — the distant signals remained at caution thereafter.

The Citadel station clock indicated 2.50 pm when the wheels of the 12.10 pm express stopped turning. After being uncoupled, the Atlantic moved forward over the points then ran back tender first to Canal shed for turning and servicing. Another epic journey was over.

Steam On The Waverley Route

In sad decay, it winds its way over Border hills and dales
Bereft of sleeper symmetry and ribbons of shining rails,
Just a ragged outline, a ragged healing sore
Weed strewn and forgotten, but rich in splendid lore.
Like the living sound of hissing steam
And clanking wagon wheels
The sad and forlorn Cheviot sheep
Taking to their heels.
The daily grind to Falahill,
The race to cross the Tweed
This gradient-littered railway line
Had "ups" and "downs" indeed!
Of beauty there was plenty,
And peace was all around
It seems that's why the smoke-filled sky
Cushioned the blasting sound
But come with me in reverie
On winter's darkest night
And hear again what I heard
When we reached for Whitrope's height.
A strong staccato loud and clear,
With constant echoing barks
Fierce white fireglow did appear
Trailing showering sparks
With the sky aglow over virgin snow,
The night had turned to day
As men worked hard (all except the guard),
The summit seemed far away.
But on guiding rail they did not quail

And their steam machine stayed strong
The great wheels turned, the hot fire burned,
And the heavy train moved on.
In silhouette the stoker's sweat
Glistened like a sparkling stream
And a knowing mate did regulate
The flow of precious steam
Then suddenly, the blasting spray
Of sparks from the engine funnel
Fell away in disarray,
Imprisoned in Whitrope Tunnel.
With thundering beat in tropical heat,
Engulfed in gaseous gloom
The engine crew were lost to view
In that hellish Border tomb.
And all around the outside ground
Was hushed in silent night
When from the pass in that barrier mass,
They emerged in fierce delight.
Spewing fire and climbing higher,
And fairly giving it socks,
As the summit appeared they loudly cheered
The sight of Whitrope Box.
A jubilant sally through Riccarton valley,
It seemed with lighter load
No need to suppress the raging express,
Streaking through Steele Road.
With the 'Distant' clear, journey's end was near
Cross the Border by Kershopefoot
But by Beeching's design, in the year '69,
Came the sad end of the Waverley Route.